THE ESSENTIAL GUIDE TO RETRO GAMING

Published in 2022 by Mortimer Children's
An Imprint of Welbeck Children's Limited,
part of Welbeck Publishing Group.
Based in London and Sydney.
www.welbeckpublishing.com

Text and design © Welbeck Children's Limited 2022
All rights reserved. No part of this publication may be reproduced, stored in a retrieval system, or transmitted in any form or by any means, electronically, mechanical, photocopying, recording or otherwise, without the prior permission of the copyright owners
 and the publishers.

The publishers would like to thank the following sources for their kind permission to reproduce the pictures and footage in this book. The numbers listed below give the page on which they appear in the book.

Shutterstock (in order of appearance): Roberto Marantan 7, 10/ sickmoose 7, 119/ robtek 7, 9, 34, 35, 119, 182/ Grzegorz Czapski 7, 34, 35/ anna__aspid 10/ J. Helgason 11/ RobertCop93 11/ Nicescene 11/ HSzone 22, JR Moreira 22/ Popartic 23/ Carlos E. Azevedo 23/ bochkaryova 23/ Matthieu Tuffet 34/ paramouse 35/ PixelChoice 35/ k_nastia 35/ VectorPixelStar 35, 118, 119 / Alexey Boldin 35/ Lenscap Photography 35/ Jfanchin 35/ Exclusively 118/ Ben Gingell 118/ POM POM 119/ Aof Kittisak 119/ Jemastock 182/ JR Moreira 182/ Interneteable 182.

Gettyimages (in order of appearance): D. Lentz 7, 183/ Jiblet 8/ Future Publishing 9, 23/ AnthonyRosenberg 183.

Every effort has been made to acknowledge correctly and contact the source and/or copyright holder of each picture. Any unintentional errors or omissions will be corrected in future editions.

This book is not endorsed, sponsored and/or has any association with Nintendo Co., Ltd, the names and logos 'Nintendo', 'Nintendo Switch' are trademarks of Nintendo Co., Ltd.. All screenshots and images of Nintendo characters/ gameplay are © of Nintendo Co., Ltd. All screenshots and images of the any other characters/ gameplay are © their respective owners.

ISBN 978 1 83935 186 0

Printed in Dongguan, China

10 9 8 7 6 5 4 3 2 1

Text and Design: Dynamo Limited
Design Manager: Sam James
Editorial Manager: Joff Brown
Production: Melanie Robertson

Disclaimer: This book is a guide and review book for general informational and entertainment purposes only and should not be relied upon revealing or recommending any specific direct secrets and methods of the game. The publisher is not associated with any names, characters, gameplay, trademarks, service marks and trade names referred in this book, which is the property of their respective owners and are used solely for identification purposes. This book is a publication of Welbeck Children's Limited and has not been licensed, approved, sponsored, endorsed by any entity or individual and does not have any association with any person or entity.

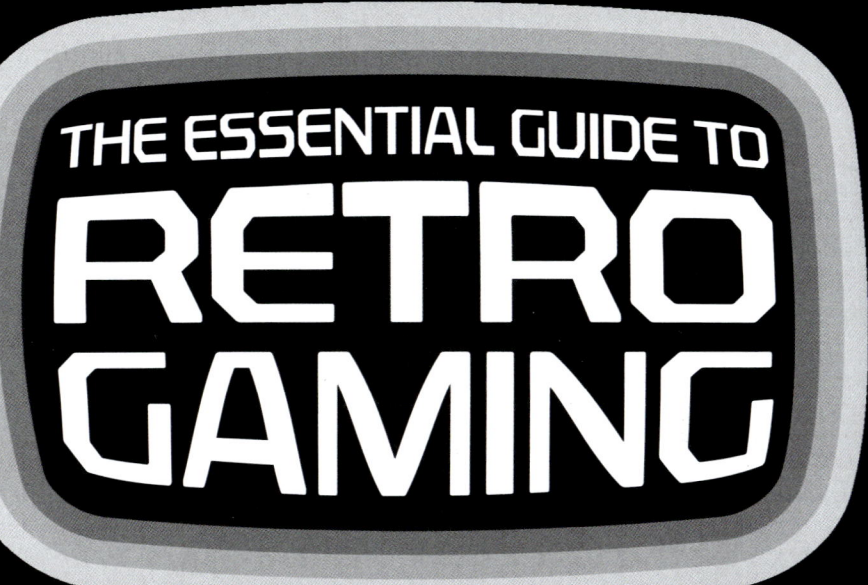

CONTENTS

READY, PLAYER ONE?	6
HONORABLE MENTIONS	8
ARCADE TIMELINE	10

ARCADE GAMES

PAC-MAN	12
DONKEY KONG	14
PAPERBOY	16
SPACE INVADERS	18
MARBLE MADNESS	20
ATARI TIMELINE	22

ATARI GAMES

ADVENTURE	24
MISSILE COMMAND	26
SUPER BREAKOUT	28
CHOPLIFTER!	30
CENTIPEDE	32
NINTENDO TIMELINE	34

NES GAMES

SUPER MARIO BROS. 3	36
THE LEGEND OF ZELDA	38
CASTLEVANIA II: SIMON'S QUEST	40
MEGA MAN 2	42
SNAKE RATTLE 'N' ROLL	44
SOLAR JETMAN: HUNT FOR THE GOLDEN WARSHIP	46
PUNCH-OUT!!	48
DOUBLE DRAGON II: THE REVENGE	50
BATMAN: THE VIDEO GAME	52
DUCKTALES	54
RETRO QUIZ!	56

GAME BOY GAMES

TETRIS	58
POKÉMON RED AND BLUE	60
WARIO LAND: SUPER MARIO LAND III	62
GARGOYLE'S QUEST 2	64
KIRBY'S DREAM LAND 2	66

SNES GAMES

SUPER MARIO WORLD	68
THE LEGEND OF ZELDA: A LINK TO THE PAST	70
SUPER METROID	72
F-ZERO	74
PILOTWINGS	76
STARFOX	78
SIMCITY	80
SUPER MARIO KART	82
SUPER SMASH TV	84
LEMMINGS	86

GAME BOY COLOR GAMES

THE LEGEND OF ZELDA: LINK'S AWAKENING	88
MARIO GOLF	90
METAL GEAR SOLID	92
DONKEY KONG COUNTRY	94
RAYMAN	96

N64 GAMES
STAR WARS
EPISODE 1: RACER 98
THE LEGEND OF ZELDA:
THE OCARINA OF TIME 100
SUPER MARIO 64 102
BANJOKAZOOIE 104
LYLAT WARS 106
SUPER SMASH BROS 108
MARIO KART 64 110
YOSHI'S STORY 112
STAR WARS: ROGUE
SQUADRON 114
TONY HAWK'S PRO
SKATER 2 116
SEGA TIMELINE 118

MASTER SYSTEM GAMES
GHOULS 'N' GHOSTS 120
SPEEDBALL 2:
BRUTAL DELUXE 122
CALIFORNIA GAMES 124
AFTER BURNER 126
ALEX KIDD IN
MIRACLE WORLD 128
ASTERIX 130
THE NEWZEALAND STORY 132
EARTHWORM JIM 134
R-TYPE 136
GAUNTLET 138

GAME GEAR GAMES
BUBBLE BOBBLE 140
SPACE HARRIER 142
DR ROBOTNIK'S MEAN
BEAN MACHINE 144
THE GG SHINOBI 146
OUTRUN 148

MEGA DRIVE GAMES
STREET FIGHTER II 150
SONIC THE HEDGEHOG 2 152
ALADDIN 154
MORTAL KOMBAT 156
STREETS OF RAGE 2 158
ECCO THE DOLPHIN 160
ANOTHER WORLD 162
TOEJAM AND EARL 164
RISTAR 166
TAZ-MANIA 168
CHARACTER QUIZ 170

DREAMCAST GAMES
SONIC ADVENTURE 172
SEGA BASS FISHING 174
METROPOLIS
STREET RACER 176
VIRTUA TENNIS 178
CHUCHU ROCKET! 180
SONY TIMELINE 182

PLAYSTATION GAMES
CRASH BANDICOOT 184
WIPEOUT 2097 186
PARAPPA THE RAPPER 188
COLIN MCRAE RALLY 190

PLAYSTATION 2 GAMES
RATCHET & CLANK 192
SSX TRICKY 194
PRO EVOLUTION
SOCCER 6 196

GAMECUBE GAMES
THE LEGEND OF ZELDA:
THE WIND WAKER 198
ANIMAL CROSSING 200
SUPER MONKEY BALL 202

GAME BOY ADVANCE GAMES
METROID FUSION 204
MARIO VS
DONKEY KONG 206
RETRO QUIZ! ANSWERS 208

READY, PLAYER ONE?

Welcome to the wonderful world of retro gaming — you're gonna love it! You may be wondering what exactly a 'retro game' is. Games your parents played? Games with blockier graphics and no online mode? They're so much more!

Retro games are a vast collection of the best and most exciting games that you've probably never played. And because there are so many of them, we're here to guide you towards the best ones and show you how you can play them without having to blow the dust off an ancient console that would be happier nestled in a museum with its other elderly electronic friends!

The consoles may not have been as powerful as the ones we have these days, but that didn't stop the developers, who cranked out classic after classic (after classic). And they are all just as playable as they ever were.

PLAYSTATION 1

GAME BOY

GAME GEAR

If you've had a glance at the contents page you'll have noticed that we mainly focus on the holy gaming trinity of Nintendo, Sega and Sony. As we mentioned earlier, the number of games from the 80s and 90s is vast. Proper vast. Too vast for us to feature anywhere near all of them, so we've focused on the best and the best known! We've also stuck to consoles that you can jam into the back of your TV, rather than the various home computers that were also popular with gamers.

NES

PLAYSTATION 3

DREAMCAST

GAME BOY COLOUR

So, player one — are you ready?

7

HONORABLE MENTIONS

We couldn't get through a whole book without mentioning a few of the lesser-known consoles. So, if you want to go further in your retro-games odyssey, then these should be on your list...

COMMODORE 64

An early entry in the 8-bit market, the Commodore 64 was a huge seller thanks to its spectacular library of games, among which were classic arcade conversion *Bubble Bobble* and the gloriously named *Zak McKracken and the Alien Mindbenders*.

ATARI ST

One of the first entries into the 16-bit market, the Atari ST was popular for its music production capabilities and for games such as *Xenon 2: Megablast* and *Dungeon Master*.

COMMODORE AMIGA

Hot on the heels of the Atari ST was this next-gen update from Commodore, with *Speedball 2: Brutal Deluxe*, *Lemmings* and *The Secret of Monkey Island* leading the charge on the gaming front.

NEO GEO

This is the best and longest-running console you've probably never heard of. Although it had some awesome games (including *Fatal Fury Special* and *Blazing Star*), the prices of them were wallet-bustingly high.

PC ENGINE

Also known as the TurboGrafx-16 in the US, the PC Engine was rather overshadowed by the twin might of Nintendo and Sega. If you're into scrolling shooters, though, you'll be in your element, as it had loads of them, including *Gradius*, *Galaga* and *R-Type*.

SEGA SATURN

Sega's rival to the PlayStation and N64 failed to really take hold due to its focus on 2D when the gaming world had very much gone 3D. It still boasts a handful of titles worth checking out, not least the thrills of *Sega Rally Championship* and the thumping *X-Men Vs Street Fighter*.

So, there you go. Retro gaming in a nutshell: Nintendo, Sega, Sony and a bunch of others. Oh, and arcades! How could we forget about them?! Turn the page to discover how the machines housed in these often dark and dingy venues kick-started a gaming revolution…

ARCADE TIMELINE

Arcade machines (also known as coin-ops, due to them requiring a steady supply of spare change to keep the gaming fun going) are essentially consoles that play one game, and are housed in a whopping great cabinet.

THE GOLDEN AGE

Late 70s to early 80s

Pac-Man! *Donkey Kong*! *Space Invaders*! The world went gaming mad, and musty arcades around the world rang out with the sound of kids' pocket money being funnelled into all manner of awesome machines.

Arcade machines often had unique controls (rollerballs, handlebars and light guns), and sometimes a handy seat (mainly for driving games) or perhaps a motorbike to straddle.

THE FORCE ISN'T STRONG IN THIS ONE

In the early 80s, before he settled on Yoda, *Star Wars* creator George Lucas considered naming his Jedi master 'Buffy' instead!

COMPETITION TIME

The 80s

With home consoles making their mark, the arcade industry came out swinging, with stunning games such as *After Burner*, *Super Hang-On* and *Outrun*.

PHONE HOME

In the early 80s a typical mobile phone weighed 2kg, could store a whopping 30 numbers and only provided you with 30 minutes of talk time per charge. How times have changed...

FISTS OF FURY

The 90s

The new decade saw the arcades dominated by thumping great beat 'em-ups, including the legendary *Street Fighter II* and *Mortal Kombat*.

KING OF KONG

If you want a glimpse into the competitive side of arcade gaming check out the 2007 film *King of Kong*. It follows school teacher Steve Wiebe as he attempts to beat the world-record high score for *Donkey Kong* that hasn't been topped for 25 years.

THE TRUTH IS OUT THERE

Popular 90s toys Furbys looked innocent enough, but many people genuinely believed they were either spying on them, teaching kids rude words, or that they could interfere with flight equipment on planes! Thankfully, none of these rumours were true.

3D AND MORE

Mid-to-late 90s

Eye-popping 3D graphics not only gave us racing gems such as *Daytona USA* and *Crazy Taxi*, but also ushered in the rhythm game craze with *Dance Dance Revolution*.

The games we cover on the following pages are all from the so-called 'Golden Age' because the advent of home consoles saw many of the later arcade classics find their way into living rooms around the world.

11

ARCADE GAMES

PAC-MAN

WHAT'S IT ALL ABOUT?

Before Mario, before Sonic, and before nearly every other iconic game character there was PAC-MAN: the yellow, puck-shaped ever-hungry maze botherer who ain't afraid of no ghost.

It's a simple life being PAC-MAN: charging around a maze, eating pellets, dodging four ghosts, occasionally chomping on some fruit, and sometimes swallowing a cheeky Power Pill so you can scoff some spooks. Once a maze is pellet-free it's on to a slightly harder one. And then another, and another, and then… you get the idea, right?

As well as coping with increasingly complex levels it's also vital you figure out how the ghosts work the mazes: Blinky (the red one) is determined to chase PAC-MAN down; Pinky (we think you can guess the colour here) is fond of an ambush; Inky (the blue lad) works with Blinky to try and force the PACster into a wrong move; and Clyde (with the fetching orange shade) generally bumbles about and legs it if our yellow friend gets too close. Trying to remember all this while hurtling around a maze is taxing at first but feels like second nature once you've cleared a few screens, and the game remains as compelling, fun and a-MAZE-ing as it ever was!

PAC-MAN, meet the ghosts – Blinky, Pinky, Inky and Clyde.

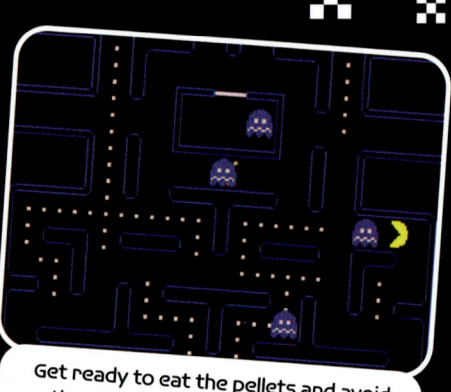

Get ready to eat the pellets and avoid the ghosts in a fast-paced frenzy!

WAYS TO PLAY TODAY

RETRO RATING 3/5

iOS and Android
Fire up your Android or iOS device of choice and download the app version of the original arcade classic to satisfy all your pellet-munching needs. And the best news? It's free!

Nintendo Switch Online
Another freebie if you're a Nintendo Switch Online subscriber. *PAC-MAN 99* is a great multiplayer update where you can slug it out online against 98 other players in a battle royale for ultimate PAC-supremacy.

RETRO RATING 4/5

RETRO RATING 5/5

PlayStation 4 and 5
Naturally, *PAC-MAN* has made his way on to the next-gen consoles. *PAC-MAN Champion Edition 2* boasts 3-D graphics, updated gameplay and a host of different play modes.

The original *PAC-MAN* is impossible to complete due to a programming quirk. You can gobble your way to the 256th level, but don't expect to clear it!

ARCADE GAMES

DONKEY KONG

WHAT'S IT ALL ABOUT?

There's trouble on the building site! A giant ape has nabbed one of the workman's girlfriends and is chucking all manner of stuff at any would-be rescuer. Welcome to the world of *Donkey Kong*.

Back in the day, Mario was known as 'Jumpman'. He spent his time leaping over barrels, dodging fireballs, clambering up ladders and never quite saving his girlfriend, Pauline, from a giant ape named Donkey Kong, who'd pick her up and lumber off to the next screen as soon as the unfortunate chap reached the top of the scaffold.

Donkey Kong was, and is, a horrendously difficult game to play (let alone master!) with expert timing needed to leap over the barrels and other assorted hazards. Casual gamers will have a tough time making it off the first screen! It takes an incredible level of skill and dedication to reach the legendary 'kill screen' (see the box on the next page), due to the often erratic way that the game lobs obstacles at you. But despite all that, it has that special quality that makes it a wildly addictive part of any good collection.

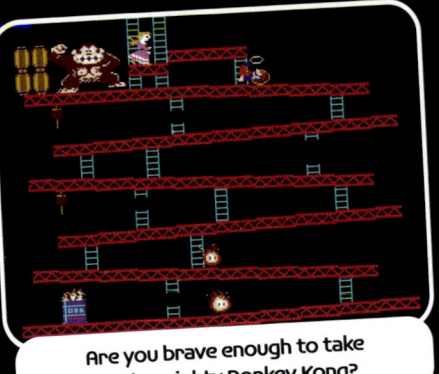

Are you brave enough to take on the mighty Donkey Kong?

Look out for hazards and obstacles at every turn!

WAYS TO PLAY TODAY

RETRO RATING 5/5

Nintendo Classic Mini

Thankfully these days you don't have to feed your spare change into an arcade cabinet and can enjoy ape-chasing japes from the comfort of your sofa. This NES recreation differs from the original in that you can complete it!

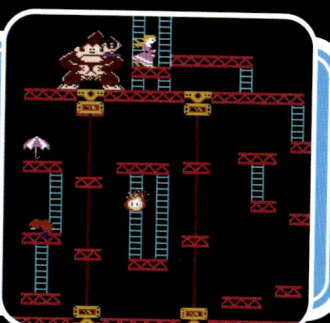

Nintendo Switch Online

As well as giving you access to the original, the retro section for Switch Online also offers up the *Donkey Kong Country* series from the SNES days. Our favourite out-of-control ape also graced many other Nintendo consoles, so keep your eyes peeled for further classic releases.

RETRO RATING 4/5

Unlike modern games, the original arcade *Donkey Kong* can't be completed. Once a player reached the 117th screen, the game froze after 4 seconds due to a programming glitch. This is famously known as a 'kill screen' and you needed to be a seriously elite player to reach it.

ARCADE GAMES

PAPERBOY

WHAT'S IT ALL ABOUT?

It's a tough life out on those mean suburban streets, and only one person has what it takes to make sure everyone gets their daily dose of news… Paperboy!

If you walked into a developer's office today and pitched a game called 'Yodel Driver' in which you simply delivered parcels, it's fair to say you wouldn't get very far. But a young lad on a bike lobbing newspapers into mailboxes and onto doormats? Gaming gold! And so it was that *Paperboy* pedalled into existence and on to arcade infamy.

To be fair, there's more to it than just the basics. As well as quickly pedalling your way through a lovely day in the neighbourhood and delivering papers to subscribers, you also have to cause as much hassle as possible to non-subscribers, and dodge classic suburban hazards such as lawnmowers, dogs and rogue tyres bouncing down the street. Sometimes ghosts even get in on the action. The gameplay and the graphics are pretty basic, but with a streak of anarchic humour added to the mix, it really delivers.

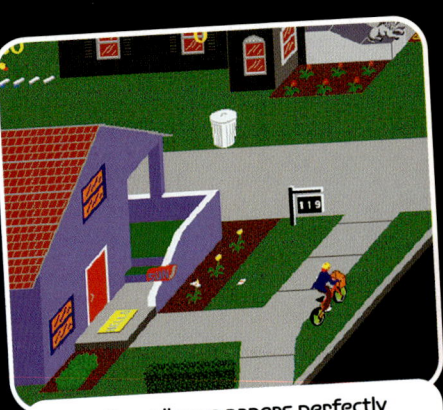
Deliver all your papers perfectly and your points are doubled!

This calls for pedal power!

WAYS TO PLAY TODAY

RETRO RATING 3/5

Xbox 360
In the years that followed its initial release, *Paperboy* popped up on a fair few consoles. But after an appearance in the App Store, the only modern system that features the cheeky scamp is the Xbox 360. It's a fairly faithful recreation, but you don't get the classic handlebars to control the action.

Instead of a joystick, the original Atari arcade machine featured a set of handlebars for you to cling on to and steer the lad to newspaper-delivering glory. Unlike on a real bike, you pushed these forwards to speed up and pulled them back to brake. There was a handy button on one side to launch each newspaper mailbox-wards.

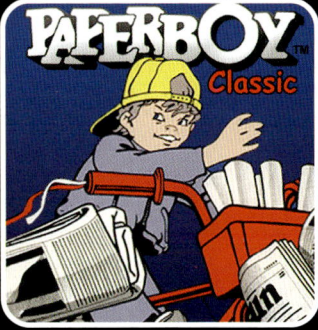

ARCADE GAMES

SPACE INVADERS

WHAT'S IT ALL ABOUT?

It's the grandaddy of alien-fighting shoot 'em-ups that inspired a generation or two of game designers (and relieved millions of kids of their allowances in the process!)

Space Invaders burst onto the arcade scene (well, we say 'burst', but 'shuffled on in tight formation' may be a better description) and quickly became the most popular game around! It went on to be the first arcade game licensed for a home console. Players took control of a laser base and were charged with blasting the alien hordes who attacked 48-at-a-time in precise columns of six. Once you'd gotten rid of them, another 48 showed up who were even more wily than the last lot.

As with most retro classics, the game hit on the magic formula of creating addictive gameplay from incredibly simple mechanics. It was so simple that you could only move your laser blaster left and right! The graphics struck a chord, too, with the blocky aliens cementing themselves into pop culture and enduring to this day.

Don't stop shooting — if the invaders reach the base of the screen it's game over!

The more aliens you shoot, the faster they move!

WAYS TO PLAY TODAY

RETRO RATING 3/5

iOS and Android

Whether you're an Android devotee or an Apple maniac there's a *Space Invaders* app for you, as TAITO has made its arcade classic available to buy on both stores to satisfy all your alien-blasting needs.

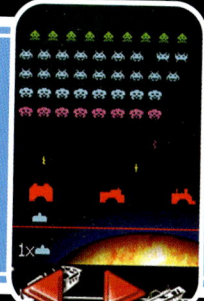

RETRO RATING 5/5

Nintendo Switch and PlayStation 4

Why have just the one version of *Space Invaders* when you can have 11? Fire up your PlayStation 4 or Switch and that's exactly what you'll get, starting with the black-and-white version through to the all-singing, all-shuffling *Space Invaders Forever*.

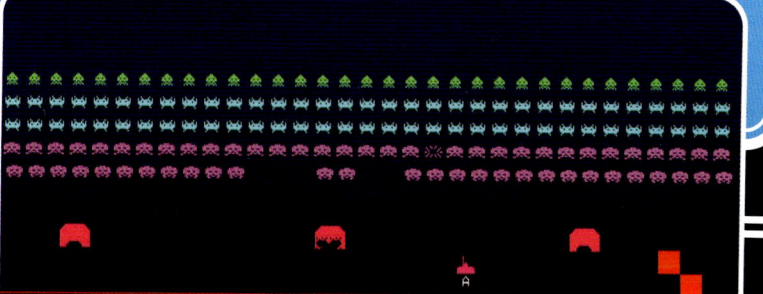

> During its initial release in Japan, *Space Invaders* was reported to be responsible for a coin shortage. People just couldn't resist pumping their loose change into the alien-zapping marvel!

ARCADE GAMES

MARBLE MADNESS

WHAT'S IT ALL ABOUT?

While other games put you in charge of heroes, armies or whopping great spaceships, Atari decided that a single, solitary marble was more than enough to be getting on with. Strangely, they were right.

If you can find another game that combines racing with the gameplay of miniature golf and levels inspired by Dutch artist M.C. Escher (look him up, kids, he's awesome!), we'd be mighty surprised. To be honest, we're amazed that just one game along these lines exists. But exist it most certainly does, and we couldn't be more grateful because *Marble Madness* is an absolute corker.

The premise is simple – guide your marble through the tricky terrain before time runs out while avoiding all manner of obstacles and hazards. Alternatively, go head-to-head (or marble-to-marble) with a mate to race (and barge) your way to the finish line. *Marble Madness* followed in the grand old arcade tradition of using non-joystick control methods, employing a trackball to steer the action (also seen on *Missile Command*, fact fans) and really get you into the marble mindset. There may only be six levels to complete, but it's too much fun to play through just once.

The controls are simple – all you need is your D-pad!

WAYS TO PLAY TODAY

RETRO RATING 3/5

Xbox One
Originally released on the Xbox 360, *Midway Arcade Origins* was added to the Xbox One via the backwards compatibility program and contains 30 classic arcade games, including *Marble Madness*. However, some of the other titles pushed the package into PEGI 16 territory, so you may have to wait a few years before getting your marble on.

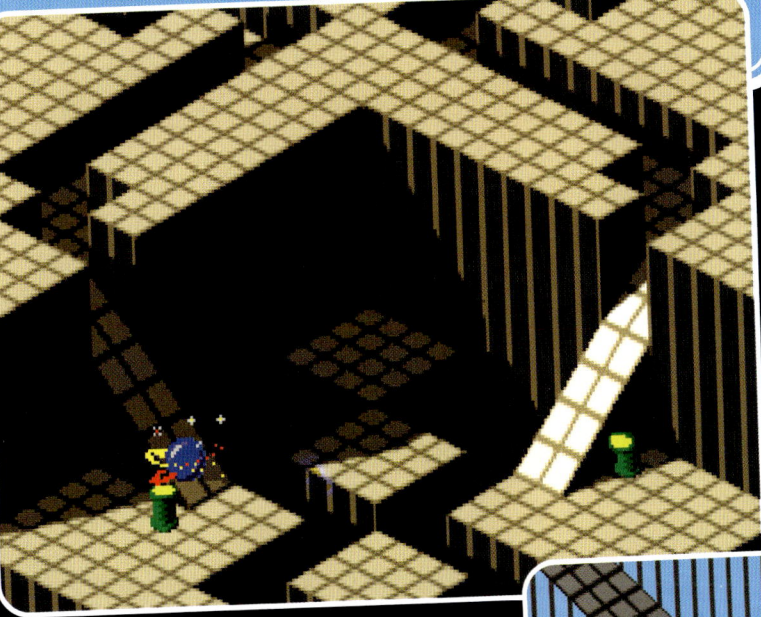

A sequel went into development in the 90s, but poor results from early tests meant it never went into production. However, 12 prototype arcade boards are thought to still exist…

ATARI TIMELINE

Before Nintendo and Sega, there was Atari. With its classic games, Atari sure made its mark on the home computing boom.

Atari 2600, 5200 and 7800

The late 70s to early 90s saw Atari's home consoles, the 2600, 5200, and 7800, capture gamers' imaginations worldwide.

1979-1992

1975

Atari Home Pong

The grandaddy of video games was released and nothing was the same again!

1984-1996

Atari ST

The Atari ST represented the company in the home computer market, pumping out a solid roster of games.

THE WEB SLINGER

As the 80s were ending, computer scientist Tim Berners-Lee created the very first web browser, laying the foundations for the World Wide Web — you may have heard of it.

ALL THE COLOURS

As consoles increased in power, so did their colour palettes. In the early days the Atari 2600 had 128 colours for developers to use, while the NES only had 56. The 16-bit era saw the Mega Drive come steaming in with 512, only to take a thumping from the SNES's 32,768! 32-bit consoles breached the million mark by quite some way and colour palettes have been massively increasing ever since.

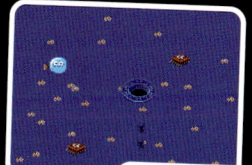

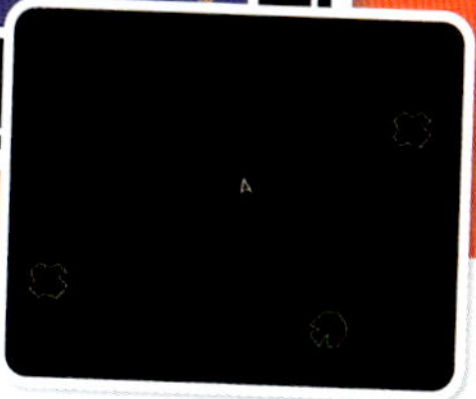

Atari Lynx
Atari got in on the handheld revolution with the Lynx, a rather nifty colour-screened unit.

1989

1993

Atari Jaguar
A valiant effort with a host of great titles, the Jaguar was another console that was swamped by the popularity of the PlayStation.

ANIMAL MAGIC

Is a real pet too much hassle? Try a digital pet – a Tamagotchi. The name comes from the Japanese for 'egg' and 'friend' and these things provided hours of simulated pet-care japes for kids in the 90s.

A PUZZLING CHANGE

The Rubik's Cube became a big hit in the 80s and is still massively popular today. The bright block got off to a tricky start as it was originally called the Hungarian Magic Cube in the late 70s. It didn't hit the big time until its legendary name change took place.

23

ATARI 2600 + 5200 GAMES

ADVENTURE

WHAT'S IT ALL ABOUT?

Long before Link roamed the top-down scrolling lands of Hyrule, there was *Adventure*. It had castles, chalices, keys, dragons and... a bat! And although you take charge of a solitary square avatar, it's a quest you'll never forget.

'Basic' is a word we'll use a lot in relation to the 2600 – especially in the graphics department. But rather than that being a bad thing, it simply meant that programmers of the time had to get super creative to conjure up engaging games. And *Adventure* provides you with a surprisingly sprawling world to roam.

Your goal is to recover the Enchanted Chalice from an evil magician and return it to its rightful place in the Golden Castle. Lined up against you are dragons (names Yordle, Grundle and Rhindle) and a bat that may or may not be in an agitated state. You can keep an eye out for objects such as keys as you explore the levels and solve puzzles. Yes, the role you play is literally that of a square, but the levels are ingenious, challenging and oddly memorable.

Find one of the many keys and unlocked castles are yours!

Remember, you can only carry one object at a time.

WAYS TO PLAY TODAY

RETRO RATING 4/5

PlayStation and Xbox

Grab a copy of *Atari Flashback Classics Vol. 2* for your console of choice and you too can flash back to this classic era of gaming. *Adventure* is faithfully recreated along with a host of other Atari titles.

RETRO RATING 5/5

Evercade

Evercade is a handheld dedicated retro games machine. It just happens to have the *Atari Collection*, which contains a cracking version of *Adventure*, among its titles.

It may not have been the first, but *Adventure* mastermind Warren Robinett popularised the 'Easter Egg' (secrets hidden within the map) in videogames. This particular one endures to this day, thanks to its appearance in the book and movie *Ready Player One*.

ATARI 2600 + 5200 GAMES

MISSILE COMMAND

WHAT'S IT ALL ABOUT?

Although fighting fire with fire is not recommended, fighting off missiles with better missiles most definitely is. It's time to take command and plunge headlong into interplanetary war!

In a time when games were largely set in fantasy worlds, *Missile Command* set itself apart by adding in a dollop of realism. The original arcade version had you defending cities from hordes of ballistic missiles, by using a trackpad-controlled cursor to knock them out of the sky with an array of weapons. The 2600 version placed the action on the planet of Zardon, fighting off the aggressors from Krytol. Much better, right?

The fictional planets help, but it's the fast and frantic gameplay that keeps you hooked. The wave after wave of attacks demand lightning-fast reflexes and pinpoint precision. The further you get into the game, the faster and more numerous the attacks become. The title may make this sound like a strategy game, but *Missile Command* is the ultimate in early shoot 'em ups.

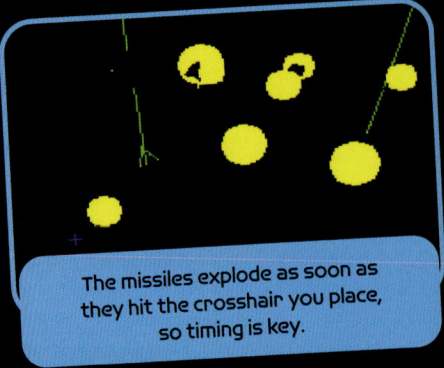

The missiles explode as soon as they hit the crosshair you place, so timing is key.

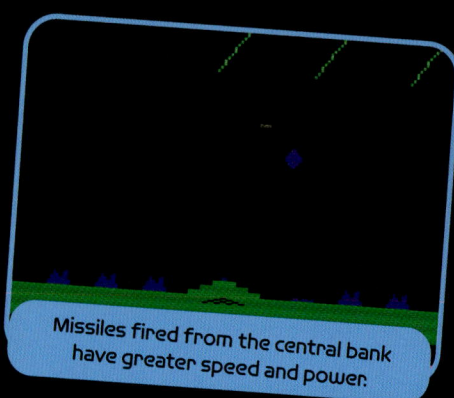

Missiles fired from the central bank have greater speed and power.

WAYS TO PLAY TODAY

RETRO RATING 4/5

aarp.org
The internet can be a bit of 'Wild West' when it comes to tracking down and playing the games of yesteryear, but there are the occasional legit blips, such as this version of *Missile Command* at aarp.org.

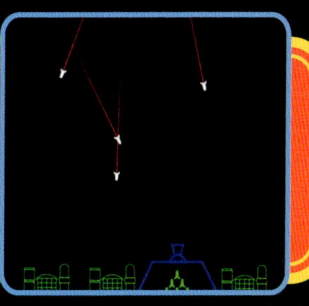

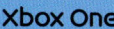

Xbox One
Jumping online with a trusty Xbox One will grant you access to a new and improved (and evolved!) version of *Missile Command*. The classic gameplay is still there, but with sound and graphics fit for the modern age.

RETRO RATING 5/5

RETRO RATING 4/5

iOS and Android
Atari has also released *Missile Command: Recharged* for mobile devices. The basic premise is still the same but the game has been totally rebuilt to make it a comfortable fit on a touch screen.

In 2011, a movie studio acquired the rights to make a Missile Command movie. But we're still waiting for it to happen!

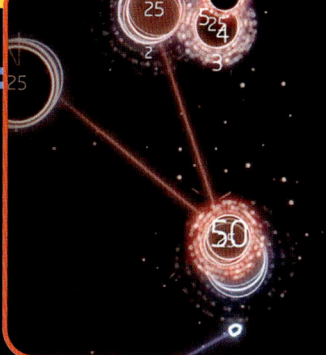

ATARI 2600 + 5200 GAMES

SUPER BREAKOUT

WHAT'S IT ALL ABOUT?

Sometimes all you need is a ball, a bouncy paddle and a never-ending supply of things to smash into in order to have a thumping good time.

Breakout was a massive arcade hit in the late 70s, so it was only a matter of time before it went 'super'. And even though the premise is simple, it really is super! You control a paddle that bounces a ball into a wall of smashable blocks. Once you've done away with one lot, it's on to another. The 'super' part of this version mainly comes from the three extra play modes: Double, where you have two balls to contend with; Cavity, where there are two balls encased in the blocks just waiting to be freed; and Progressive, where the blocks gradually move down the screen, adding that extra bit of pressure.

It's fair to say that *Super Breakout* is not hugely varied in terms of gameplay, but what it does do it does spectacularly well. Smashing blocks takes hold in much the same way as the falling blocks in *Tetris* do and provides hours of destructive fun.

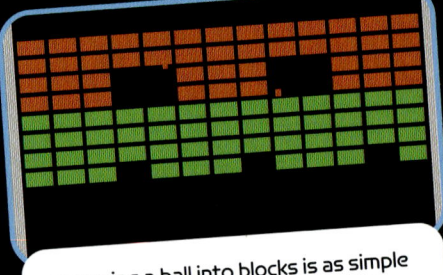

Bouncing a ball into blocks is as simple as gaming gets. And it's insanely fun!

WAYS TO PLAY TODAY

RETRO RATING 4/5

iOS
There are a fair few pretenders floating around in the mobile app world but if you want the real thing, fire up your Apple device and head to the App Store for *Breakout Boost*. Atari's fab update features all manner of enhanced graphics, sound and playability.

RETRO RATING 5/5

Xbox One and PlayStation
The ever-reliable *Atari Flashback Classic* series features *Super Breakout* in its original form and with added multiplayer and online modes.

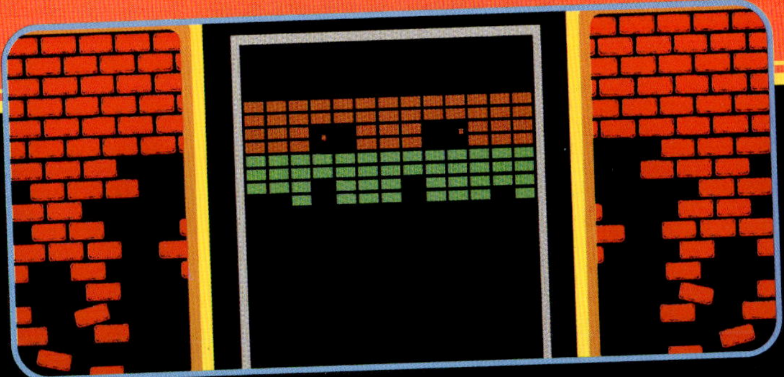

Apple supremo Steve Jobs was hired by Atari to build a prototype of *Breakout*. He stayed up for four days straight with fellow Apple legend Steve Wozniak to finish it.

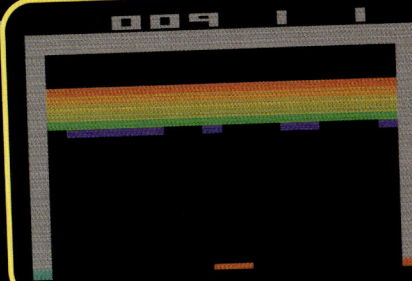

ATARI 2600 + 5200 GAMES

CHOPLIFTER!

WHAT'S IT ALL ABOUT?

It's time to strap in and get to the chopper in this ace shooting and hostage rescuing game.

Ready to take the controls of a helicopter and rescue hostages from the evil 'Bungeling Empire'? *Choplifter* is a whole lot of helicopter fun.

One of the main appeals of *Choplifter* is the ability to fly the helicopter in one direction while shooting in another, which is a simple idea that elevates the game no end. It also requires a good deal of precision, as unlike the frenzied blasting of *Missile Command*, your mission isn't just to shoot the bad guys - it's to rescue the hostages as well. This means not shooting them while you try to take out the various enemy vehicles firing relentless pot-shots at you — it's full-on multitasking mayhem!

Remember, you can only shoot at the enemies when you're in the air.

The modern update has some truly tricky rescues to deal with.

30

WAYS TO PLAY TODAY

RETRO RATING 3/5

Xbox One
There is an HD remake on the Xbox 360 but sadly the updated graphics and gameplay landed it with a 16 rating. And despite the numerous Atari bundles showing up over the years, *Choplifter* in its original form has so far been absent from all of them. So far, anyway...

In the early 80s a good portion of games were converted from arcade machines. *Choplifter* has the rare distinction of having started life on home consoles before being elevated to coin-op status.

ATARI 2600 + 5200 GAMES

CENTIPEDE

WHAT'S IT ALL ABOUT?

It's usually aliens that need a good blasting, but insects are kind of like aliens, right? Now that's sorted, let's get shooting!

On the surface *Centipede* sounds like a challenge that can be beaten without too much effort. You must take control of a bug blaster and do away with a centipede as it winds its way down the screen towards you, weaving through a field of mushrooms. But the reality is far more ingenious and devilish. Shoot an end segment of the centipede and that's one bit gone, but take a pot shot at a middle segment and you suddenly have two centipedes to contend with. Plus there are all manner of other beasties to dispose of at the same time, with spiders, fleas and scorpions all vying for the attention of your blaster.

Rather than being an open field (like in *Missile Command*), it has mushrooms strewn around the game area, making it trickier to get effective shots off. They can be destroyed – it just takes four shots per 'shroom! All of the distractions make it a hectic game, but it's so satisfying when you finally get to show those garden marauders who's the bug-blasting boss.

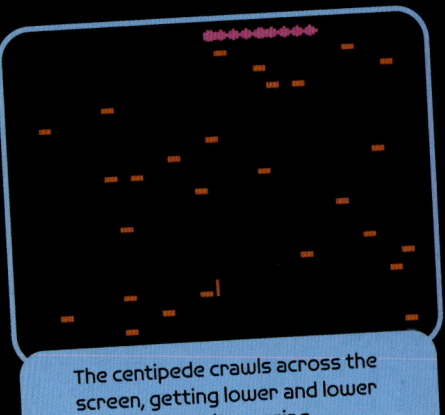

The centipede crawls across the screen, getting lower and lower with each crossing...

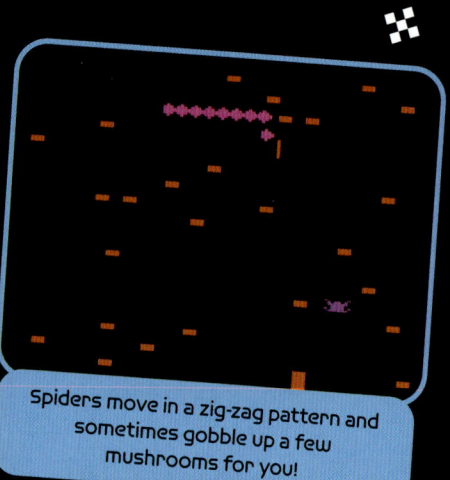

Spiders move in a zig-zag pattern and sometimes gobble up a few mushrooms for you!

WAYS TO PLAY TODAY

RETRO RATING 4/5

App Store
Another handheld App Store exclusive, *Centipede* is available to slither on to whichever Apple mobile device you favour. It offers the magic combination of classic gameplay and updated graphics.

Xbox One
If you're not an Apple superfan but are a Microsoft devotee, you're in luck! *The Centipede Recharged* is up for download on the Xbox network, boasting various new power-ups and all-new creative challenges.

RETRO RATING 5/5

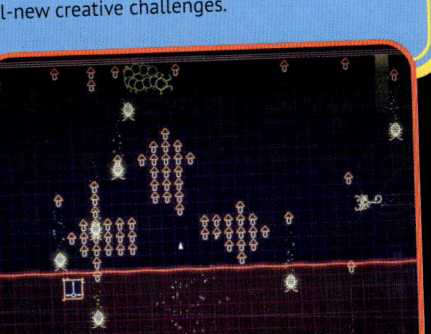

? Although it's not immediately apparent, you actually play a gnome in *Centipede*. And in the mid-80s a *Dungeons & Dragons*-style board game emerged in which you could play as both the gnome and the centipede!

33

NINTENDO TIMELINE

The story of everyone's favourite Japanese game company!

Game Boy
A NES in your pocket but with slightly ropey black-and-white dot-matrix graphics. Awesome games, though.

1989

1985

Nintendo Entertainment System
And so it begins... The NES is released onto an unsuspecting public and a gaming revolution explodes.

1990

Super Nintendo Entertainment System
As the new decade kicked off, the NES got a super upgrade with the arrival of the Super NES.

FIRST UP #1
The very first NES games available were *Donkey Kong*, *Donkey Kong Jr.* and *Popeye*.

Did you know that the SNES looked different in different territories?

OLD VS NEW

Computing power has obviously increased over the years, but by how much? Well, a classic NES has a processor speed of 1.66MHz and just 2KB of onboard RAM (although this jumps up with a game cartridge in). And an average iPhone? 3100MHz (3.1GHz) and around 4,000,000KB (4GB) of RAM.

2KB RAM VS 4GB RAM

Nintendo 64

With Sony trying to nab the gaming crown, Nintendo came out swinging with the N64 and some of the greatest games of all time.

1996

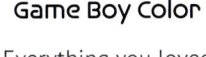
1998

Game Boy Color

Everything you loved about the original Game Boy but now in colour. Black-and-white graphics were officially a thing of the past.

MUSIC ON THE GO

In the pre-iPod, pre-smartphone days it was popular to lug around a boombox to blare out some bangin' tunes. The downside? They generally weighed around 11 kilos and ate up batteries!

CHEER UP!

In 1982 computer science professor Scott Fahlman created the very first emoticon in order to stop messages being misunderstood on college networks. His creation? :-)

BRICKIN' IT

Search engine giant Google was launched in 1998 and was so popular it eventually became a verb. In the early days when money was tight, head honchos Larry Page and Sergey Brin partially housed their first storage server using LEGO. It's safe to assume they don't do that now!

35

NES GAMES

SUPER MARIO BROS. 3

WHAT'S IT ALL ABOUT?

Super Mario Bros. introduced Mario, Nintendo's most famous character… and Mario's third NES adventure is an all-time classic.

Put simply, this is the best NES game ever – and we'll fling a turtle shell at anyone who disagrees! The story here is standard Mario fare – Bowser and his Koopalings have taken over the Mushroom Lands and only an Italian handyman and his brother can stop them (if you're new to this world, Bowser does this a lot). But that's by the by, as it's the action that counts and this is jam-packed with intricately designed levels that are a constant joy to explore and conquer.

Super Mario Bros. 3 takes everything that's fantastic about the first two games and ramps it up. With new sub-games and mini-quests, five new power-ups (including a racoon suit that enables Mario to take flight or turn into a statue in a way that your average raccoon most definitely cannot) and stunning graphics, you're immediately drawn in by the superb playability that combines fiendish puzzles and ultimate platform mastery. There are eight worlds to complete and each one is rounded off with a ruck with a Koopaling until you reach Bowser himself for a final one-on-one showdown. This sure isn't a quick game to complete but it's worth every second.

The gang's all here! It wouldn't be a Mario game without a new assortment of enemies!

WAYS TO PLAY TODAY

RETRO RATING 5/5

Nintendo Classic Mini

Released back in 2017, the NES Mini came packed with 30 classic games, of which *Super Mario Bros. 3* was one – faithfully recreated down to the last pixel. NES Minis are in short supply these days so keep your eyes peeled for a secondhand bargain.

RETRO RATING 5/5

Nintendo Switch Online

There's a great library of classic games available at Switch Online including *Super Mario Bros. 3*. All you need is a Switch Online Membership. (Oh, and a Switch. But you knew that, right? Good, we knew we could count on you.)

? The game opens and closes with a theatre curtain rising and falling, which prompted a fan theory that the story was meant to be a play. Amazingly this was later confirmed by the creators to be true!

37

NES GAMES

THE LEGEND OF ZELDA

WHAT'S IT ALL ABOUT?

Buckle up — we're off on an adventure to Hyrule, a magic land that's constantly under threat from various evil-doers who are (surprise, surprise) up to no good.

Link the elf has one very distinct pastime – saving the land of Hyrule. In this first outing he's tasked with reassembling the Triforce of Wisdom, saving Princess Zelda and defeating the evil prince of darkness, Ganon. Quite a tall order for a young elf, we think you'll agree. But thankfully he's quite a plucky lad and handy with a sword, so off he goes...

The gameplay takes a top-down perspective as you travel the sprawling, detailed and multi-directional land of Hyrule. The controls are simple to master and although the combat elements may not look like much, they're hugely satisfying and challenging. There's a massive area to explore, with numerous dungeons nestled below the ground just waiting to reveal their secrets, along with some truly fiendish puzzles to solve. This is all topped off with impressive graphics and a suitably atmospheric soundtrack. *The Legend of Zelda* is indeed a legendary game.

As well as exploring there's plenty of fighting for Link to take care of too!

Hyrule also includes subterranean dungeons with secrets to discover...

WAYS TO PLAY TODAY

RETRO RATING 5/5

Nintendo Switch Online
The Legend of Zelda was part of the first wave of retro games that crashed onto the Switch on launch day. And rightly so. *Zelda II: The Adventure of Link* is also available if you fancy sampling a quest in a side-scrolling form.

Nintendo Classic Mini
Both games are included in the console reissue and, well, what more is there to say? They demand your attention and your controller. Grab your shield and sword and get adventuring – Princess Zelda isn't going to save herself!

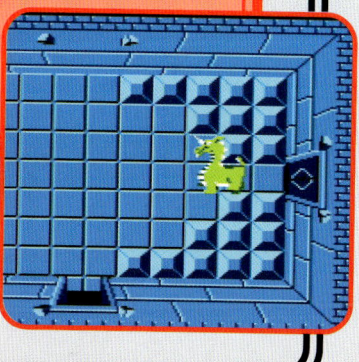

RETRO RATING 5/5

? Most NES cartridges came in a fairly drab-looking grey colour, but not *The Legend of Zelda*. Link's iconic adventure came in shiny gold. Although the vast majority are not worth anywhere near their weight in actual gold, a sealed, early production version did sell for a whopping $870,000 in 2021!

NES GAMES

CASTLEVANIA II: SIMON'S QUEST

WHAT'S IT ALL ABOUT?

Count Dracula's lads are all fired up and ready to cause trouble. Luckily, Simon Belfont is on a quest to put them in their place (the graveyard).

Simon has been sent on a quest to cut a swathe through the undead hordes of Transylvania and find Count Dracula's five missing body parts in order to lift a curse that's been placed on him. All in a day's work for an ace vampire hunter. Not all the inhabitants are hostile – there are a few helpful villagers who need to be sought out to give you some vamp-hunting tips and the odd handy weapon upgrade.

As well as being a top-notch platform actioner with as many ghouls and as much action as the NES's 8 bits of power can handle, *Simon's Quest* has role-playing elements and non-linear gameplay. Plus, it has a 'day and night' system that means the beasties are even harder to splatter once the sun goes down. It's ace searching mansions and castles and leaping from platform to platform in a gothic-tinged world. So tool up, and get questing.

Search the mansions to find Dracula's body parts!

Enemies drop hearts to collect once they've been clobbered. Use them to boost your health or buy new whips.

WAYS TO PLAY TODAY

RETRO RATING 5/5

Nintendo Classic Mini
Another no-show for the dedicated retro section at Switch Online. But fear not as Mr Belfont is very much a part of the NES Mini, along with as many undead minions as you can shake a whip at.

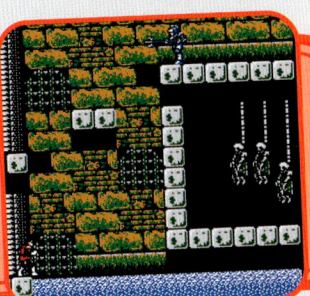

RETRO RATING 4/5

PlayStation 4, Xbox One and Nintendo Switch
Castlevania II has been included as part of *Konami's Castlevania Anniversary Collection*. As well as this particular quest, you can also follow the Belfont lad across his many escapades on other classic consoles such as the SNES, Game Boy and Mega Drive.

? The credits for the game include loads of amusing made-up names based on actors and characters from classic horror movies. The only downside is that all the fake names mean it's not clear who actually created the original *Castlevania*!

NES GAMES

MEGA MAN 2

! WHAT'S IT ALL ABOUT?

He's a man. He also happens to be mega. Yes, it's Mega Man! Often under-looked in the pack of famous NES platform games, this is a tricky beast to get to grips with but worth every second of your mega time.

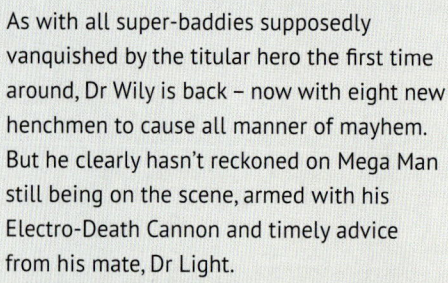

As with all super-baddies supposedly vanquished by the titular hero the first time around, Dr Wily is back – now with eight new henchmen to cause all manner of mayhem. But he clearly hasn't reckoned on Mega Man still being on the scene, armed with his Electro-Death Cannon and timely advice from his mate, Dr Light.

Although there's plenty of villain-blasting action to be had, the main element of the gameplay is the puzzle-solving, as the levels are brilliantly inventive. They often leave you scratching your head, convinced there's no way through, when suddenly you see the solution. The difficulty of the game is almost perfectly balanced, meaning that you get that little bit further on each play. There's also plenty of combat to be had thanks to the presence of some memorable baddies who need taking down. Mega, indeed.

The gameplay is fast-paced and includes plenty of head-scratchers to figure out (although obviously not on this bit!).

Mega Man leaps into the modern age with this awesome update.

WAYS TO PLAY TODAY

RETRO RATING 5/5

Nintendo Classic Mini

Alas there's no *Mega Man* on Switch Online (boo!) but he is very much present and correct on the NES Mini reissue (yay!), where you'll find him in all his requisite mega glory.

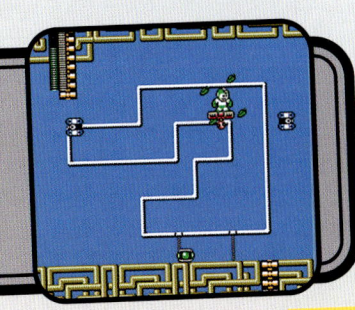

RETRO RATING 4/5

PlayStation 4, Xbox One and Nintendo Switch

Old Megs has been through many different reincarnations over the intervening years – the most up-to-date is *Mega Man 11*, where our hero is still (still!) dealing with Dr Wily and his devilish schemes. The graphics have had a major upgrade since the NES days, but the 2D platform action is still as thrilling as ever.

? The original *Mega Man* game wasn't exactly the solid gold hit that was expected. The sequel you see here was reluctantly given the green light with little-to-no expectations that it would become an ongoing franchise. How things change!

SNAKE RATTLE 'N' ROLL

WHAT'S IT ALL ABOUT?

Join snake friends Rattle and Roll in their quest to dodge sharks, avoid an oversized foot and duck the attentions of living toilet seats to consume any and all Nibbly Pibblys in sight.

There are loads of truly bonkers levels to conquer, all packed with humour and eye-popping 3D graphics. As you progress, the routes to the exits get ever-more complex as you leap and eat your way around the checker-board landscape while avoiding some of the most inventive baddies you'll ever encounter. Did we also mention that to complete each level, the snakes have to eat Nibbly Pibblys aplenty until they weigh enough to trigger a bell at the top of some weighing scales? No? This is just one of many things that makes *Snake Rattle 'n' Roll* one of the oddest and most fun platform games around.

And there's a super-fun two-player mode as well where the snakes race to scoff the most Nibbly Pibblys and pack on the pounds the fastest. It's more fun than you can shake a snake at!

Be careful, as Nibbly Pibbly dispensers can also chuck out bombs!

Exit the levels by triggering the bell on the weighing scales.

WAYS TO PLAY TODAY

RETRO RATING 4/5

Xbox One
Snake Rattle 'n' Roll slithered onto our screens thanks to Brit developers Rare. This means it can be played on the Xbox One by firing up a copy of *Rare Replay*, where you can also sample its snake-tinged speedboat-racing classic, *Cobra Triangle*.

? When one of the snakes drops into the water and is pursued by a shark, the soundtrack quotes the famous theme song from the movie *Jaws*.

45

NES GAMES

SOLAR JETMAN: HUNT FOR THE GOLDEN WARSHIP

WHAT'S IT ALL ABOUT?

Slow-paced space exploration with realistic planetary gravity sounds like a real old yawn-fest. But Solar Jetman is star quality personified and demands that you strap in to join in his search for the Golden Warship...

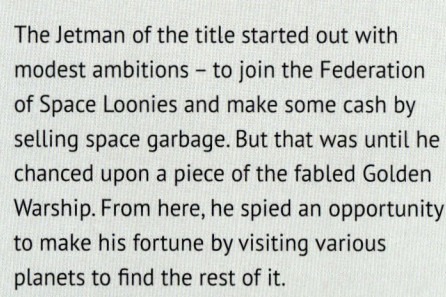

The Jetman of the title started out with modest ambitions – to join the Federation of Space Loonies and make some cash by selling space garbage. But that was until he chanced upon a piece of the fabled Golden Warship. From here, he spied an opportunity to make his fortune by visiting various planets to find the rest of it.

The gameplay is simple – explore each world, dodge guns and alien beasties, and tow the latest piece of Warship back to base. But there's way more to it. The physics of how the ship moves vary with the gravity settings of each planet! The levels are also densely designed environments that provide hours of interstellar exploration fun. Couple this with great graphics and sound, and you have a game that is out of this world.

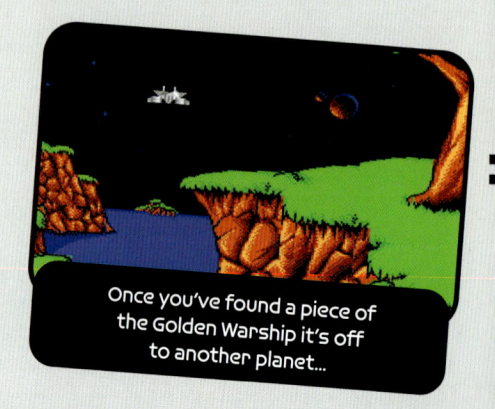

Sustain too much damage to your pod and you're left with just your spacesuit.

Once you've found a piece of the Golden Warship it's off to another planet...

WAYS TO PLAY TODAY

RETRO RATING 4/5

Xbox One

Fire up the Xbox One and grab yourself a copy of *Rare Replay*, the 30-game 30th-anniversary celebration of legendary developer Rare. You can also get to grips with *Jetpac* and *Lunar Jetman*, the first and second instalments in the series that first appeared on the ZX Spectrum back in 1983.

?

Programmer Ste Pickford has said that the movement of Solar Jetman's pod was inspired by the way a scuba diver moves. However, this inspiration came from playing an old Spectrum diving game rather than getting out on the high seas with a tank and mask!

NES GAMES

PUNCH-OUT!!

WHAT'S IT ALL ABOUT?

A game so exciting they had to put two (count 'em!) exclamation marks in the title, this boxing sim certainly packs, well, a punch. And a jab. And an uppercut.

Like all good boxing tales, *Punch Out!!* follows the story of a small rookie with big dreams as he takes on the toughest sluggers around. In this case it's Little Mac with his faithful trainer Doc Louis, who's out to take down the big 'uns of the boxing world, such as King Hippo, Soda Popinski and the aptly named Super Macho Man.

Sport sims on the NES were always a mixed bag, with that mix being mainly made up of mediocre to really quite bad titles (we're looking at you, *Kick Off*). But *Punch-Out!!* broke the mould, with one swift knock-out blow. Rather than being a side-on affair, the third-person perspective puts you squarely behind Little Mac so that you're properly facing down your opponents. And rather than going at them in a hail of mindless button mashing, you need quite different strategies to get each opponent on the canvas for a ten-count. Glove up, and get swinging.

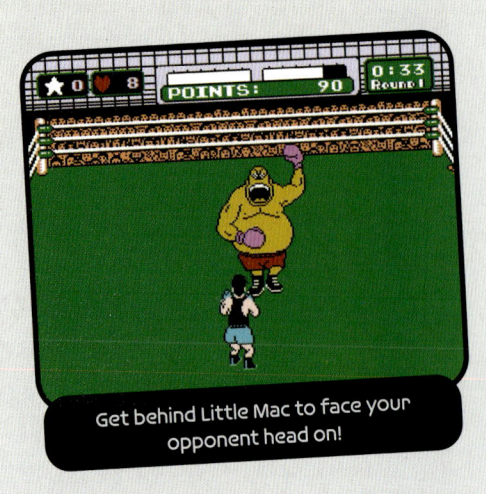

Get behind Little Mac to face your opponent head on!

Watch out for Von Kaiser's jaw-rattling uppercut!

48

WAYS TO PLAY TODAY

RETRO RATING 4/5

Nintendo Switch
The original arcade smash version can be purchased for the Switch via the *Arcade Archives* if you want the full retro option for your boxing capers.

RETRO RATING 4/5

Nintendo Switch Online
Super Punch-Out!! was an absolutely ace sequel released for the SNES that you can get your be-gloved hands on at Switch Online.

RETRO RATING 5/5

Nintendo Classic Mini
Punch-Out!! also graces the NES reissue, where you can batter the rogue's gallery of opponents in full 8-bit retro glory.

? *Punch-Out!!* was originally named *Mike Tyson's Punch-Out!!*, but the deal to use Tyson as a character had run out by the time the game was released on the NES. So the former champ's name was simply dropped from the title.

NES GAMES

DOUBLE DRAGON II: THE REVENGE

WHAT'S IT ALL ABOUT?

Meet Billy and Jimmy! They're as mad as hell and they're not going to take it any more in this double-the-fun sequel to the all-time classic street-based fighting game.

Nintendo certainly went out of its way to position itself and its consoles as family friendly. And why not? No reason why young nippers and grizzled veterans alike shouldn't enjoy the same game. So it's a bit of a surprise to find a title like *Double Dragon II: The Revenge* lurking around on the NES and filled with all manner of punching, kicking, chain-swinging, baseball bat-wielding and knife-chucking action.

The game follows the exploits of martial arts supremos Billy and Jimmy Lee, who are out for revenge on the Black Warrior gang after they rudely shot Billy's girlfriend, Marian. The levels are the usual side-scrolling affair any NES gamer will be used to, but *Double Dragon II* sets itself apart with the inventiveness of the action as the brothers roam the streets and batter the many members of the Black Warriors daft enough to get in their way. The two-player mode is particularly good, with the lads able to hook up for some double-teaming baddie bashing (hence the title). A definite high-point of NES beat 'em-ups.

The brothers team up to take down a boss in this Nintendo Switch remaster!

WAYS TO PLAY TODAY

RETRO RATING 4/5

Nintendo Switch
Once again, *Arcade Archives* is your friend, as both *Double Dragon II* and the original *Double Dragon* are available to play. Is that double the fun or quadruple the fun? Answers on a postcard!

RETRO RATING 5/5

Nintendo Classic Mini
If you can track one down, then *Double Dragon II* is also included on the mini NES reissue. Alas, *Double Dragon* is not – and thankfully *Double Dragon III* isn't either, as the third instalment somehow managed to be a poor shambling excuse of its former self.

?

In 1994 a *Double Dragon* movie was released. And in keeping with almost all video-game movies that emerged during the 90s (too many to list here), it got terrible reviews and failed to rake in the cash.

NES GAMES

BATMAN: THE VIDEO GAME

WHAT'S IT ALL ABOUT?

Holy 8-bit platform action, Batman! Take control of the Dark Knight as he cleans up the mean streets of Gotham and gives the Joker and his henchman a taste of his Batarang!

Before Batman began, before he hooked up with Robin (in the ropey movies of which we don't speak), and before he spent almost an entire film complaining about his dodgy back and creaky bat-knees, he starred in a super-stylish instalment where he took on a more cartoon-y version of the Joker. And that's what has been converted into this endlessly enjoyable side-scrolling platform-and-baddie-punching game we see before us.

The gameplay follows the 80s flick as closely as an 8-bit title can, with Batman striding down the avenues and alleyways of Gotham, taking in the Axis Chemical plant and a handful of other locations before his showdown with the Joker on the top of Gotham Cathedral. There are some nifty bat-based weapons on offer, and although they don't include the iconic grappling hook, the caped lad has a nifty 'wall jump' move where he leaps up and boosts off a wall to reach the higher platforms (this is a pretty vital move to get to grips with). Although the game isn't the most challenging when compared with other classic NES platformers, it's incredibly atmospheric and provides you with all the bat-based fun you could ever want.

An unfortunate henchman who's about to eat some Bat-fist!

WAYS TO PLAY TODAY

RETRO RATING 4/5

Nintendo 3DS, Xbox One and PlayStation 4

Although the NES *Batman* remained where it was, there have obviously been many other games released over the years featuring the Caped Crusader. Out of all the modern offerings the most similar is probably the superb *LEGO Batman* series, which can still be picked up for the 3DS, Xbox One and PlayStation 4.

? As well as the Joker, Batman also has to face off against a host of other lesser-known-but-no-less-deadly DC villains, including Deadshot, Maxie Zeus and Heatwave.

NES GAMES

DUCKTALES

WHAT'S IT ALL ABOUT?

An elderly duck and his multi-purpose walking stick may not seem like the most obvious choice for a main character, but as we've had a plumber called Mario and some bloke named Simon, why not?!

Old greedy guts Scrooge McDuck never passes up an opportunity to increase his already humungous fortune. And what better way to do that than to indulge in some globe-trotting adventures to root out and collect some more treasure? You take control of the elderly quackster and guide him round mines, mountains, jungles, castles and the moon to nab his five treasures.

Although the game only presents you with what seems like a miserly five levels of platform adventuring, they're challenging and enjoyable enough to keep you coming back for one more play. The character of Scrooge himself is also immense fun to control as he runs, jumps and ducks (haha) his way through the various eye-catching locations, using his cane as a pogo stick or as a bat to give baddies a swift smack in the chops. You'd be 'quackers' not to give this one a whirl!

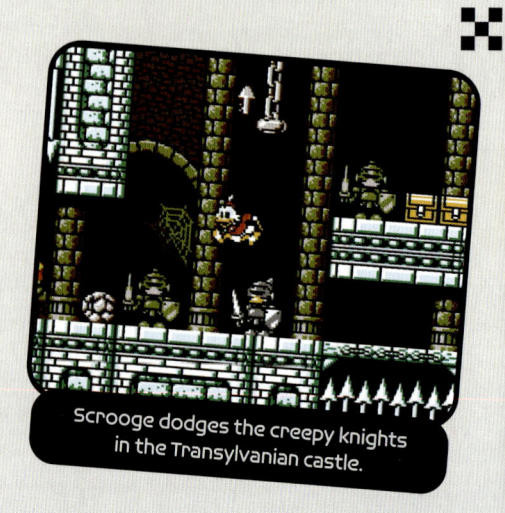

There's great variety in the action, with Scrooge shimmying up vines in the Amazon level.

Scrooge dodges the creepy knights in the Transylvanian castle.

WAYS TO PLAY TODAY

RETRO RATING 5/5

Xbox One, PlayStation 4 and Steam

After decades without a rerelease, everyone's favourite miserly duck popped up in *The Disney Afternoon Collection*, where *DuckTales* nestles alongside five other ace games.

RETRO RATING 5/5

Xbox One, PlayStation 4 and Steam

If you prefer your ducks to be all shiny and new-looking, then point your webbed feet in the direction of the *DuckTales: Remastered* version of Scrooge McDuck's classic adventure.

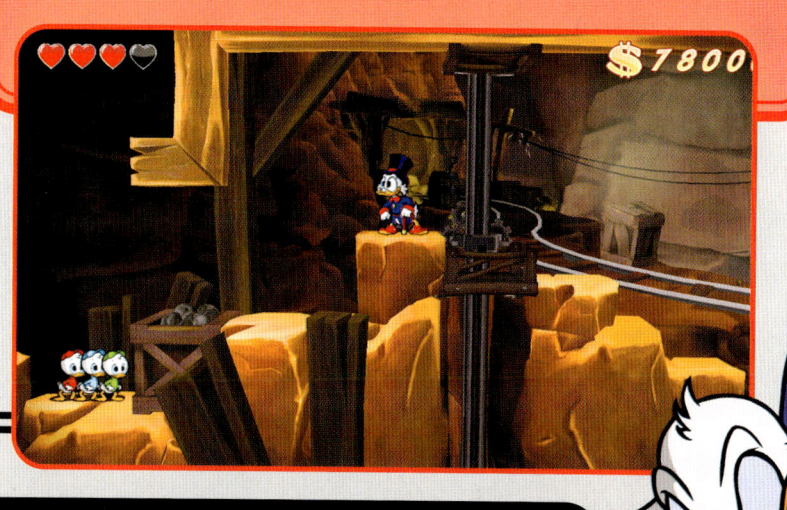

?

As mentioned, Scrooge McDuck's walking stick has more than one use. The best is when you jump in the air, hold Down on your D-pad, and turn it into a pogo stick. This is super-handy for bouncing over larger gaps and squishing some undesirables, too.

RETRO QUIZ!

Think you know your retro stuff? Test your knowledge with these multiple-choice questions and then flip to the back of the book to see how you did. Ready?

1
In *Paperboy*, the titular delivery lad encounters some unexpected baddies in his neighbourhood. Which of the below does NOT put in an appearance?

a. A ghost
b. A street dancer
c. The Rock

2
In the classic Atari fave *Adventure*, what is the main character that you control?

a. A square
b. A hexagon
c. A triangle

3
In *The Legend of Zelda*, what is Zelda's role in the land of Hyrule?

a. Prime Minister
b. Princess
c. Legendary DJ

4
Which Pokémon has a name that sounds a bit like a sneeze?

a. Pikachu
b. Pik-a-tissue
c. Pik-a-bleurghh!!

5
What CAN'T you throw at your fellow competitors during a race in *Super Mario Kart*?

a. Banana skins
b. Turtle shells
c. Shade

6
In the mega-popular N64 platform game, what is the name of the bear that hangs around with Kazooie the bird?

a. Banjo
b. Ukelele
c. Mandolin

7

Which arcade game is named after a type of glove?

a. *Big Foam Finger*
b. *Mitten*
c. *Gauntlet*

8

Sonic the Hedgehog gained a two-tailed fox friend in the second incarnation of his Sega Mega Drive game. What was his name?

a. Tails
b. Shoulders
c. Knees and Toes

9

Which relaxing water-based hobby was the basis for a smash-hit game on the Sega Dreamcast?

a. Bass fishing
b. Swan bothering
c. Shopping-trolley spotting

10

PaRappa is the star of an ace PlayStation game. But what does he do? Is he:

a. A dancer
b. A YouTuber
c. A rapper

11

Which GameCube game involves rolling a medium-sized furry animal around inside a big ball?

a. *Super Chimp Crisis*
b. *Super Primate Panic*
c. *Super Monkey Ball*

12

What planet does Samus Aran visit in *Metroid Fusion*?

a. Earth
b. SB388
c. The Big Spooky Planet of Death

13

Which of these is NOT a playable character in *Star Wars Episode 1: Racer*?

a. Toy Dampner
b. Blibby Blab-blub
c. Bozzie Baranta

14

In *Ghouls 'n Ghosts* what does Sir Arthur end up having to wear when he gets struck by an enemy weapon?

a. A hat that says, 'Make Medieval Knights Great Again'
b. Just his pants, and nothing else
c. A 'Keep Calm and Quest On' T-shirt

Find the answers on page 208

GAME BOY GAMES

TETRIS

WHAT'S IT ALL ABOUT?

It's raining geometric shapes, hallelujah! Tetris took the gaming world by storm and remains not only the best game to emerge from Russia but one of the best puzzle games ever!

Even the finest games have their critics, but you'd be hard pushed to find anyone to say something negative about *Tetris*. Sure, they may let out a few rude words if their near-perfect run comes to a crashing halt but they'll be back for more. More falling blocks. More completed lines. More of the simple-yet-hopelessly-addictive gameplay.

Tetris is another one of those games that's incredibly straightforward... basic, even. A variety of differently shaped blocks fall steadily from the top of the screen and your job is simply to move them around and flip them about so they fit neatly together. Once you've formed a perfect line it disappears leaving room for more of the tumbling Tetrominoes. The more lines you clear, the higher your score, and the game also accounts for the difficulty of finished lines. One line gets you 100 points. But 4 lines in one go? 400 points and eternal glory! (Maybe not the second part.) *Tetris* also has that rare distinction of being a game that can't be completed. One of the best games ever, and it will never end — what more could you want?!

Flip the block around and jiggle it left and it will fit in nicely, ready for the next one to fall...

WAYS TO PLAY TODAY

RETRO RATING 4/5

iOS and Android
Tetris has gone touchscreen with snazzy graphics and sound. There are also a number of ways to play that include daily challenges, Survival mode and the ability to take on your mates.

RETRO RATING 5/5

Nintendo Switch Online
Plump for the original Game Boy version or try one of these ace upgrades – *Tetris Effect: Connected*, *TETRIS 99*, *Puyo Puyo Tetris 1+2* or *Tetris Party Deluxe*. All come with eye-popping graphics and fab twists on the classic gameplay.

RETRO RATING 5/5

PlayStation 4 and Xbox One
You'll be hard pushed to find a better-looking version of *Tetris* than the one that graces the mighty PS4 and Xbox One. As well as an online challenge mode, there's also a multiplayer cooperative option for all you comrades out there.

? *Tetris* creator Alexey Pajitnov originally designed the game as a way to make computers seem less intimidating. Wasn't that nice of him?

GAME BOY GAMES

POKÉMON RED AND BLUE

WHAT'S IT ALL ABOUT?

Here's where it all began, with the Pocket Monsters making their way onto gaming screens worldwide and sparking a phenomenon to rival Mario, Link and Sonic combined.

If you've never encountered any of the 901 species of Pokémon (and that figure may very well have increased by the time you read this), it can be a slightly daunting prospect to take your first steps into this world. And that's why the Game Boy version of this role-playing classic is such a perfect starting place, with its far more manageable 151 creatures and gentle introduction into the pocket monsters' world.

You take the role of Ash. He's been inducted into the world of Pokémon after an encounter with Professor Oak, a famous Pokémon researcher, who pits you against his son and fellow aspiring Trainer. And then it's off into the wild to hunt for the pocket monsters. In single-player mode the gameplay has two basic elements: capturing and training your Pokémon and battling other Trainers and their own Pokémon.

It's not all aggro between Trainers, though, as a switch to multiplayer mode enables you to play against your friends and trade creatures. The game is huge and hugely fun, with so much to explore and a host of mini-quests to complete. And yes, over 151 creatures who demand that you trap them all.

It's time to get out into the wild and find those Pokémon!

WAYS TO PLAY TODAY

RETRO RATING 4/5

Nintendo Switch
Pokémon Legends: Arceus is the latest version to land on the Switch. It places the standard Pokémon-collecting fun in a huge open world to explore however you want.

RETRO RATING 5/5

iOS and Android
Pokémon GO may just be the best mobile game ever, as it brings everyone's favourite pocket monsters into the real world and connects you to gamers worldwide.

RETRO RATING 4/5

Nintendo Switch
Pokémon Brilliant Diamond and *Shining Pearl* combine everything that has made the series great up to now along with awesome new features. Winning!

? The designer of the *Pokémon* series, Satoshi Tajiri, drew inspiration from his childhood hobby of insect collecting.

61

WARIO LAND: SUPER MARIO LAND III

WHAT'S IT ALL ABOUT?

It's topsy-turvy time in the Mushroom Kingdom as Wario takes centre stage and brings his own unique flavour to the leaping and coin-collecting genre.

Usually, each successive game in the Mario series sees our plumber friend return for more action in an upgraded universe, but not here! After taking a right good thumping in *Super Mario Land 2: 6 Golden Coins*, it's lead baddie Wario who gets to return with a game of his own. He also wants a castle of his own and so sets out to Kitchen Island to get his mitts on a statue stolen by the Brown Sugar pirates to fund his grand designs. While Wario can run, jump and stomp around the various levels, he can also access different attack modes depending on what hat he's wearing (these are hidden in pots that are strewn around each level).

Although they almost share a name, Wario is not Mario, and neither is his game the same. Although there are striking similarities, the overall gameplay involves a completely different platform character who takes a fair bit of getting used to if you happen to be a seasoned Mario veteran. But it's time well spent as the challenges, puzzles and bosses are endlessly imaginative and compelling.

Although he's a different character and this is a different game, there's still plenty of leaping and coin collecting to be done!

WAYS TO PLAY TODAY

RETRO RATING 5/5

Nintendo 3DS
If you have a 3DS, you'll be able to play Wario's adventures on the ever-helpful handheld console.

RETRO RATING 4/5

Nintendo Switch
Rumours abound that the Game Boy library could start to make its way to Switch Online soon (maybe by the time you read this it almost has). But for now you can get your Wario fix from *WarioWare: Get It Together* on the Switch, which boasts over 200 ace mini games.

? Rather than just being a result of flipping a capital 'M' upside-down, Wario's name is a combination of 'Mario' (obvs!) and *'warui'*, which is the Japanese word for 'bad'.

GARGOYLE'S QUEST 2

WHAT'S IT ALL ABOUT?

The Game Boy isn't short on epic quests, and they don't come much more epic than this journey into the multiple worlds of ghosts, ghouls, gargoyles and other things beginning with 'g'…

We've all been there: you take a day off from the Ghoul Realm to go and train in an alternate dimension and when you get back, BAM!, your village has been destroyed by The Black Light and you have to figure out why. The 'you' in this case is Firebrand, his village is Etruria, and the aforementioned Black Light is the central mystery that demands a resolution.

At its core this is a terrific RPG game, with all the brain-twisting puzzles and quirky side-characters that you'd expect to encounter in an adventure like this. *Gargoyle's Quest* also chucks in a ghoulish curveball in the form of side-scrolling levels that are much more action-based and take you into the darker corners of this fantastical realm. Firebrand can also pick up an inventive range of weapons and abilities to help fend off various demonic rapscallions and propel him into places that regular gargoyles can't reach. Put together, the action, exploration and puzzle solving are perfectly balanced, making this one hell of a devilish adventure.

The original game saw Firebrand save the Ghoul Realm from Breager, the Destroyers' king!

WAYS TO PLAY TODAY

RETRO RATING 5/5

Nintendo 3DS
If you prefer your ghost and goblins to be in black-and-white and slightly blockier, you can also buy the original *Gargoyle's Quest* – featuring the adventures of Firebrand and his demonic pals – for the 3DS.

RETRO RATING 3/5

Nintendo 3DS
Gargoyle's Quest II also appeared on the NES but with slightly different gameplay, and it's this version that has had the dust blown off it and been made available for the 3DS.

? If you're a hardcore retro gamer, you may well recognise ol' Firebrand, as he had a prominent role in the classic medieval actioner *Ghosts 'n Goblins*, where he was known as the Red Arremer.

GAME BOY GAMES

KIRBY'S DREAM LAND 2

WHAT'S IT ALL ABOUT?

As soon as you think you've seen all the cute and cheerful characters that Nintendo has to offer, you always find there's just one more. Like this one – readers, meet Kirby.

It seems that Dream Land has taken a turn for the nightmarish! The seven Rainbow Bridges that connect the Rainbow Islands have been nabbed by the King Dedede, who's been possessed by Dark Matter that's turned him into a right royal wrong'un. But never fear because Kirby is here to leap about the various platforms to save the day, helped along by his animal chums.

Most video-game characters have some sort of special ability, but we'd happily wager our monthly games budget that this is the only outing in which 'inhaling' is a super-power. Quite how this was settled upon is anyone's guess, but it's utterly ingenious! Inhale air and mash the jump button and Kirby is flying. Inhale and swallow an enemy and the Kirb-ster gains their ability. Choose to gob the baddie out and a hail of stars sweeps away objects in your path. It really is a masterstroke and brings a fresh and exciting feel to the standard platform japes. Take a breath, and drift off to Dream Land at your earliest opportunity.

Kirby may be small, but he has BIG adventures!

WAYS TO PLAY TODAY

RETRO RATING 4/5

Nintendo Switch Online
Kirby's next outing popped up in full 16-bit glory on the SNES, which features the same classic Kirby action, only better! Check it out via the Expansion Pack on Switch Online.

Nintendo Switch
Kirby is so successful these days that he has his own Kirby Hub on Switch Online with all manner of games available. *Kirby Fighters 2* is a corker, and *Kirby and the Forgotten Land* should be with us by the time you read this!

? If you want to 100% complete the game, then after each boss battle you have to re-enter the level and play a mini game that revolves around catching stars. 100%-ing the game opens up more gameplay options…

SNES GAMES

SUPER MARIO WORLD

WHAT'S IT ALL ABOUT?

If you thought *Super Mario Bros. 3* was good, you ain't seen nothing yet! Here the Italian lads come smashing on to the Super NES in a blaze of coins, mushrooms and Krazy Koopa Kritters...

It's a good thing that Mario and Luigi enjoy saving the Mushroom Kingdom so much, because — surprise, surprise — Bowser is back for yet more aggro. But rather than his return from banishment in the mountains being tediously inevitable, it's an absolute joy! It means you get to spend hours and hours and hours in an upgraded Mushroom Kingdom, exploring yet more perfectly designed levels and solving satisfying puzzles. It also marks the debut of Yoshi, Mario's dinosaur buddy who gives the plumber a ride on his back while chomping his way through the various beasties.

The game is a challenge-and-a-half and no mistake, with 96 levels to discover and conquer. These include levels within levels, the bonkers mind-bending physics of the Ghost Houses and the 'only experts need apply' Star Worlds. And throughout all of this is an array of visual gags and an incredible level of ingeniousness. Although Nintendo saved the machine-stretching giant leap forward for *Super Mario 64*, this is still very much an upgrade on the previous NES version and it's absolutely essential you play it.

Yoshi gains different abilities depending on the type of Koopa he gobbles up.

WAYS TO PLAY TODAY

RETRO RATING 5/5

Nintendo Switch Online
Super Mario World is literally at the top of the list of reissued SNES games and deservedly so. It also loses none of the fantastic detail when shrunk down onto your Switch screen for handheld play.

RETRO RATING 5/5

Super Nintendo Classic Edition
Tracking down *Super Mario World* on a SNES reissue also puts you in possession of its sequel/prequel, *Yoshi's Island*. Here you take control of the daring dino and help Baby Mario rescue Baby Luigi from Baby Bowser.

RETRO RATING 5/5

Nintendo Switch
If you like your Mario games with 'World' in the title, then check out *Super Mario 3D World*. This fab instalment recently popped up on the Switch in all its 3D glory.

? In the original Japanese version of *Super Mario World*, Yoshi had the ability to eat dolphins! Curiously this wasn't carried over to any of the other releases.

SNES GAMES

THE LEGEND OF ZELDA: A LINK TO THE PAST

WHAT'S IT ALL ABOUT?

Link is back (which is handy because Princess Zelda is once again gone) and an adventure across the vast land of Hyrule is beckoning our hero from his bed on a dark and stormy night…

There are two things you could always rely on when buying a Nintendo console – it will have a new Mario game and a new Zelda game. And both will be awesome. Link's previous outing on the NES had been a side-scrolling affair that somehow didn't really feel right, and so the return to a top-down view is most welcome, as we follow Link in his attempt to free Princess Zelda and the land of Hyrule from an evil wizard who's hell-bent on releasing the demon king and former foe, Ganon.

Role-playing games are often thought of as slow-paced and more measured affairs, but *A Link to the Past* bristles with fast-paced action as Link hurries from one side of the sprawling map to the other, fending off castle guards and descending into the depths of multi-level dungeons. The game is also gorgeous to look at, with bags of atmosphere as Link forges his way through heavy rainstorms and negotiates the 'Dark World'. If you're after a compelling story with more action than you can shake an elven sword at, this is the game for you.

Interacting with other characters is a vital part of a successful quest.

WAYS TO PLAY TODAY

RETRO RATING 5/5

Super Nintendo Classic Edition

As with the NES Mini, Nintendo ceased production of the SNES reissue a while back. But if you keep a watch on your local secondhand games emporium, you'll more than likely see one pop up for sale, already loaded with Link's ultimate 2-D top-down outing.

RETRO RATING 5/5

Nintendo Switch Online

Let's once again say a big thank you to the gaming gods for the existence of Switch Online, as for the price of a membership you can take Link and his adventures with you wherever you go. Link may only have made a single appearance on the SNES, but it's one you don't want to miss.

? *A Link to the Past* features a number of Zelda firsts – the first appearance of Kakariko Village, the first visit to Lake Hylia and the first time we see an ocarina...

SNES GAMES

SUPER METROID

WHAT'S IT ALL ABOUT?

And now for something completely different. Well, perhaps not completely, but *Super Metroid* certainly is a different beast to the usual bright-coloured family fare found on the SNES.

On the surface this is a standard side-scrolling space-set action-adventure romp. You take control of Samus Aran and guide her around the planet Zebes in order to find an infant Metroid that's been nabbed by Ridley, her arch nemesis and the dastardly leader of the space pirates. So far, so fine. But *Super Metroid* is so much more. The levels are fantastically detailed and complex, with the subterranean settings rendered in dark foreboding graphics that put you right into the grimy and ominous sci-fi universe that's been set up in the stonking intro sequence. Combined with the music it creates an atmospheric experience that's unrivalled on the SNES.

The gameplay is top-notch too, with plenty of power-ups on hand to modify Samus Aran's suit and provide her with new ways to move – all of which are vital for making it through to the next part of the game relatively unscathed. You owe it to yourself to get hold of this immersive masterpiece.

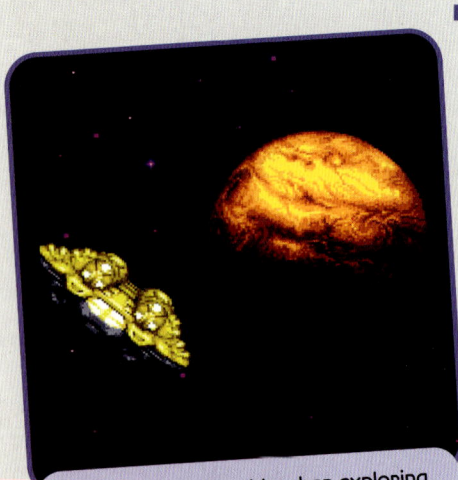

If you get into trouble when exploring, the ship can be used to replenish Samus Aran's health.

WAYS TO PLAY TODAY

RETRO RATING 5/5

Super Nintendo Classic Edition
Super Metroid was also bundled with the SNES reissue along with a host of other 'Super' games from the 16-bit console. If you liked *Metroid*, you knew you were going to like the sequel, simply because it was like *Metroid* but 'Super'.

Nintendo Switch Online
Unsurprisingly *Super Metroid* was firmly among the first wave of SNES games unleashed onto the retro section of Switch Online. Here it sits alongside the rest of the all-time greats from that era. You can also hop over to the NES page and check out the original.

RETRO RATING 5/5

? For fans of the later *Metroid* games (particularly *Metroid Prime*, arguably the other high watermark in the series) it may surprise you that *Super Metroid* was originally intended to be the last in the series. And Nintendo didn't return to the *Metroid* world until eight years after its release.

SNES GAMES

F-ZERO

WHAT'S IT ALL ABOUT?

F1? Pah! This is *F-ZERO*, a racing series Lewis Hamilton and his petrol-head pals can only dream of. Strap in and prepare to take on the fast and the furious of the future...

F-ZERO is set in the future. Waaay in the future. 2560 to be precise! This is a time when Earth-dwellers have been engaged in intergalactic trading and the resulting technological innovations mean they can produce super-fast cars that hover a few feet above the ground rather than using those old-fashioned tyre things. And, of course, once you have a super-cool ride you have to take it racing and prove you're ace enough to make it to the top step of the podium.

Funnily enough, *F-ZERO* has a fair bit in common with *Mario Kart* in that there are various power-ups located on each track that are vital to locate in order to win big (that's where the similarities end, though, as this is a touch more serious). The gameplay is suitably swift and futuristic, and your rivals have different racing tactics that take a fair bit of skill to overcome. You can never have too many racing games, especially when one of those could be *F-ZERO*.

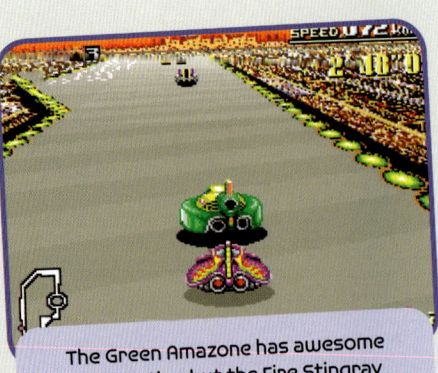

The Green Amazone has awesome acceleration but the Fire Stingray has a higher top speed — which will you pick?

Replenish your energy by taking a dash through the Pit Zones.

74

WAYS TO PLAY TODAY

RETRO RATING 5/5

Nintendo Switch Online
All your futuristic racing thrills and spills can be accessed with a Switch Online Membership. Although it's worth keeping in mind that *F-ZERO* is one of the few racing games that lacks a multiplayer mode.

RETRO RATING 4/5

Super Nintendo Classic Edition
If you're a retro purist and insist upon only playing these games in the way Nintendo originally intended, the SNES reissue has you covered, with everyone's favourite 2560-set racing game ready and waiting to be fired up.

?

As well as being the main character here, Captain Falcon (driver/pilot of the aptly named Blue Falcon) was almost co-opted into being the launch mascot when the SNES was first thrust upon the gaming world. He also later popped up in the thumping *Super Smash Bros* series.

SNES GAMES

PILOTWINGS

WHAT'S IT ALL ABOUT?

It's time to take flight into the wild blue yonder and discover what a blast it can be taking on the day-to-day training involved in becoming an ace pilot.

Most flying games tend to be about shooting some other magnificent men in their flying machines and avoiding the same fate yourself. Not *Pilotwings*, though. This is about nothing more than soaring through the cool, clear air in the most controlled way possible and earning your various pilot licences in the disciplines of light plane, sky-diving, hang-gliding and rocket belt (which doesn't include extra marks for Tony Stark impressions, alas).

A lot of work has gone into recreating the physics of flight and it really shows.

A lightness of touch on your control pad is very much the order of the day here, with pinpoint accuracy and consistency the things that garner the highest rewards. If this sounds a little too serious, then fear not, as success in the various events opens up some great bonus levels, such as bouncing a winged man across a series of trampolines and guiding a diving penguin into a pool (we're happy to be corrected, but it's unlikely your average pilot is trained in this way). Earning your wings has never been so fun.

Being ace at falling is every bit as important as being great at flying.

Steady flight and a smooth landing are the core skills you need to conquer *Pilotwings*.

WAYS TO PLAY TODAY

RETRO RATING 5/5

Nintendo Switch Online
If you arm yourself with a membership then all your plane-related needs can be met at the Switch Online store. Which is handy as *Pilotwings* was a notable absence from the SNES Mini reissue.

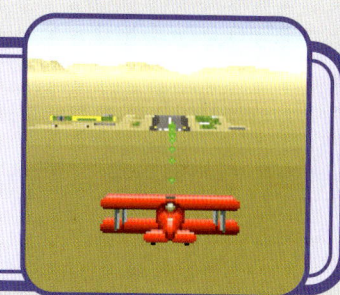

RETRO RATING 4/5

N64 and Nintendo 3DS
If you have a secondhand emporium nearby, or a family member who hoards their old consoles, then *Pilotwings* has some great sequels that you could check out. The N64 boasts *Pilotwings 64* (obviously) and *Pilotwings Resort* touched down on the 3DS.

? Such was the popularity of the *Pilotwings* tunes that six tracks were included as part of the Nintendo Super Famicom Game Music album that was released in Japan in the early 90s.

SNES GAMES

STAR FOX

WHAT'S IT ALL ABOUT?

Rather than sniffing round your bins and creating an almighty racket in the dead of night, this fox is out to save the galaxy from the forces of evil, one laser blast at a time.

This is very much the flip-side to *Pilotwings*. Think fast-paced action, futuristic settings, and all manner of lasers and blasters at your disposal. Oh, and there's a fox at the controls! Set in the fictional Lylat System, Fox McCloud and his mates Falco Lombardi, Peppy Hare and Slippy Toad (yes, really) must defeat evil scientist Andross and his army. And luckily they have an ace up their sleeve – the super high-performance Arwing craft.

The gameplay is essentially standard fare, with you taking control of Fox McCloud and his Arwing while blazing a trail of destruction through any unfortunate baddies. You're also accompanied by the other three members of the team in console-controlled crafts, and your score at the end of each level takes into account how well you defended your teammates. *Star Fox* was one of the games that was designed to show off the SNES's capabilities, and it still impresses. The combat is fantastically thrilling with ace sound and graphics to match. This is absolutely one fantastic fox.

You can use thrusters and retro rockets to speed up and slow down your Arwing.

Keep an eye out for your mates – they'll either be chasing a baddie or being chased themselves!

WAYS TO PLAY TODAY

RETRO RATING 4/5

Nintendo Switch Online and Super Nintendo Classic Edition

Not only can you play *Star Fox* through the the usual sources, you can also get your mucky paws on *Star Fox 2*. This was unreleased at the time but has seen a new lease of life via these retro routes.

RETRO RATING 4/5

Nintendo Wii U

Star Fox Zero is the sixth game in the series and is ready for you to play should you have a Wii U to hand (or paw).

? Originally the SNES and N64 versions were named *Star Wing* and *Lylat Wars*, respectively, due to issues with an existing company called 'StarVox'. These now appear to have been resolved, which led to the name changes on the rereleases.

SNES GAMES

SIMCITY

WHAT'S IT ALL ABOUT?

Become the master of all you survey with the ultimate in world-building frolics. Yes, this really is a game where you enter the profession of town planning and experience local bureaucracy for fun...

While most of the games we've featured so far have been action-packed to varying degrees, *SimCity* is far more relaxed and is one of the finest examples of an easy-going game. Which is as it should be, because town planning (what you're doing here) is most definitely a slow process. But that's not to say that it's dull – far from it! Constructing and managing your own urban paradise is oddly gripping and challenging.

SimCity presents you with a blank canvas and an array of buildings and infrastructure to place on what is essentially a living and breathing map. Certain things will bring in money, some will garner positive public approval, while others won't – it's all about managing these things while growing your newly created town (well, city – this game isn't called *SimTown* after all). If you're ever feeling burnt out from the constant assault of other livelier games, then kicking back in *SimCity* is the most relaxed time you'll ever spend in front of a console.

Get ready to unleash your best urban-planning moves!

Make decisions and develop your city.

WAYS TO PLAY TODAY

RETRO RATING 3/5

iOS, Android and Amazon
Released in late 2014, *SimCity BuildIt* is a spinoff from the original that's available on your mobile device of choice. The gameplay differs in a few ways but it's still a great way to exercise all your city-building dreams.

PC
If you want something with more features and on a grander scale, there are various versions of *SimCity* available on the PC, as well as a number of ace expansion packs.

RETRO RATING 4/5

? If you've been looking at the 'Sim' part of the title and wondering whether it's related to global mega-smash *The Sims*, you'd be right! *Sims* designer Will Wright was the brains behind *SimCity* and its many sequels.

SNES GAMES

SUPER MARIO KART

WHAT'S IT ALL ABOUT?

The inhabitants of the Mushroom Kingdom leave behind their platform-based japery and head to the racetracks to burn some rubber, chuck some shells and strategically drop some banana skins...

Up to this point Mario and the gang had a fairly narrow gaming existence, mostly taking on scaffold-dwelling giant apes or anyone daft enough to cause a ruck in the Mushroom Kingdom. But everyone needs a change in direction once in a while, and what could be more fun than heading to the go-kart track? At its heart, this is a nuts-and-bolts racing game with eight characters to choose from and a host of different modes and scenarios to blast you around the track.

What sets this apart are the elements imported from Mario's platform games. Not only are there numerous power-ups to nab but you can also use various items to set traps or simply lob at your opponent. And in the ace two-player mode there's nothing quite like sending your mate spinning off just before the checkered flag with a well-aimed turtle shell. Strap in, rev up and get racing.

Mario takes the chequered flag at Koopa Beach!

Track your opponents' progress on this handy map.

WAYS TO PLAY TODAY

RETRO RATING 4/5

Nintendo Switch Online
Not only can you access the classic original on your Switch, you can also play online against your mates – as opposed to the old days when you'd all have to be in the same room!

RETRO RATING 5/5

Super Nintendo Classic Edition
Here's further proof of just what a great purchase the SNES reissue is! This essential Nintendo racer is of course included and you can play with an original-design controller, just as the great Shigeru Miyamoto intended.

Strange as it may sound, it's sort of possible to play *Mario Kart* for real. Yup, if you're the right age and have the right licence, there are companies that let you tour the streets of Tokyo in a go-kart. Dungarees and a luxurious moustache are optional.

SNES GAMES

SUPER SMASH TV

WHAT'S IT ALL ABOUT?

We're familiar with those people who'll do anything to get on TV, but you ain't seen nothing yet when it comes to the shows of the future. Here it's guns, guns, more guns and deadly androids that are the order of the day.

You may think reality TV today has gone too far, but *Super Smash TV* proves there's a way to go yet. Set in the near future, you take control of a contestant who's been brave (or daft) enough to sign up for a go on Smash TV. The aim is simple – stay alive! But the hordes (and we mean hordes) of murderous robots that come streaming into each game arena make this a challenge! At the end of each single-screen level you get to fight off one of the super-tough bosses who have names such as Mutoid Man and Mr Shrapnel.

The game makes great use of the SNES controller – the D-pad moves the contestant and the four buttons fire your weapon in a particular direction. It's so simple that you can just switch off your brain and revel in the chaos. That doesn't mean it's easy – even seasoned veterans find it tough to make it to the end. But it's worth sticking at it, as we're struggling to think of a better blaster.

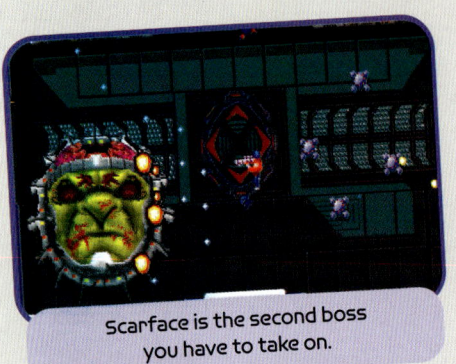

Scarface is the second boss you have to take on.

Facing off against the imaginatively named green clubbers and magenta clubbers!

WAYS TO PLAY TODAY

RETRO RATING 4/5

PlayStation 3 and Xbox One

This is another rare case of a true classic that's missing from Switch Online. However, its appearance elsewhere could be the reason for this, as it forms part of the excellent *Midway Arcade Origins* compilation, which can be played on the PS3 and Xbox One (as long as you're old enough not to be excluded by the 16 rating).

?

The original arcade machine had a 'Pleasure Dome' bonus level for when you finished the game. However, so confident were the programmers that noone would do so, the machine was shipped without it. When gamers did complete the game (and complained at the lack of reward) the level was added back in.

SNES GAMES

LEMMINGS

WHAT'S IT ALL ABOUT?

Seeing your screen fill up with hairy rodents would be a nightmare for many of us, but somehow that alarming concept forms the basis of a quite brilliant puzzle game...

Lemmings sees you take the part of a sort of rodent overlord or god and plays on the common misconception that the furry little creatures have a death wish that they carry out together. And as strange concepts go, this is a real corker and makes for a totally unique game. The set-up is this: the lemmings enter the single-screen level and you have to alter the landscape to guide as many as possible to safety (and then on to more jeopardy!). This is done by assigning a limited amount of characteristics to a certain number of lemmings so that they can dig, bomb, climb, float, block, build, bash and mine their way out to freedom, and lead the others with them.

This is a good old-fashioned puzzle game where there's very little need for D-pad dexterity and expert timing, and every need for exercising the old grey matter. Assigning the various tasks takes careful thought and one slip-up can easily lead to chaos, with hordes of the green-haired critters barrelling into a hopeless situation and just making things worse. (Although there is a handy 'nuke' option so that you can wipe the slate clean and start again). It's possibly the best rodent-based game ever.

Levels come in four difficulty groups: Fun, Tricky, Taxing and Mayhem!

WAYS TO PLAY TODAY

RETRO RATING 3/5

iOS and Android

Lemmings is yet another classic game that has found its way onto your phone. Fire up the App Store or Google Play and you can take the clueless creatures with you wherever you go.

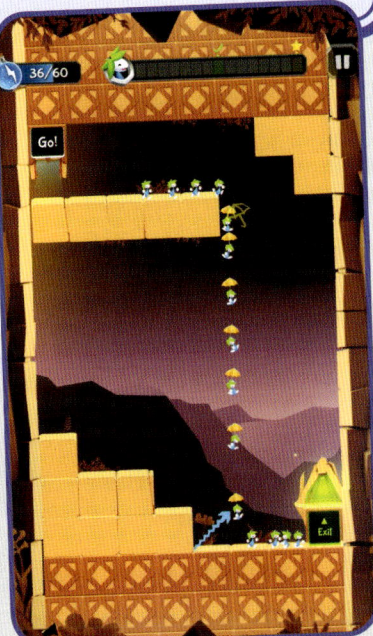

> Legendary fantasy author Terry Pratchett was reportedly a huge fan of *Lemmings*. So much so that he deleted it from his computer as it was consuming so much of his time.

THE LEGEND OF ZELDA: LINK'S AWAKENING

WHAT'S IT ALL ABOUT?

Say bye-bye to both Hyrule and Princess Zelda, as it's time for Link to broaden his horizons and sail away to new lands and new adventures…

Everyone needs to get away once in a while, even elves. And Link's working holiday brought a freshness to the series while retaining all the things that gamers loved about following the inquisitive chap on his various quests. *Link's Awakening* sees our hero wash up on the shores of Koholint Island after his boat is caught in a storm. After chatting with a mysterious talking owl, Link establishes that the only way off the island is to awaken The Wind Fish. And so the crusade begins…

The game keeps the classic top-down view while also chucking in the occasional side-scrolling mini quest in a tip of the hat to *The Adventure of Link* on the NES. The gameplay is neatly balanced between exploring the landscape and acquiring new items, taking on the occasional baddie in armed combat, solving puzzles and descending into the odd subterranean dungeon. And while the stories in previous games were occasionally over-serious, *Link's Awakening* seamlessly blends in a healthy dose of fun and whimsy. It's well worth tagging along for the ride.

You never know what you're going to find in the dungeons!

WAYS TO PLAY TODAY

RETRO RATING 4/5

Nintendo Game & Watch
A few years ago Nintendo rebooted their classic Game & Watch device and released two versions: Mario and Zelda. The Zelda unit not only houses *Link's Awakening*, but also *The Legend of Zelda* and *Zelda II: The Adventure of Link*.

RETRO RATING 5/5

Nintendo Switch
Although the original version isn't available in the retro online section, you can get your hands on an upgraded 3D version that has an absolutely stunning new graphics style.

? Before becoming an official part of the *Zelda* series, *Link's Awakening* started out life as a side project by the developers, which they did just for the fun of it.

89

GAME BOY COLOR GAMES

MARIO GOLF

WHAT'S IT ALL ABOUT?

What do plumbers do to relax and get away from all the stresses, strains and rampant Koopalings of the Mushroom Kingdom? That's right, they head to the fairway in some natty trousers for a spot of golf.

As well as his usual platform antics, Mario has always had a good line in extra-curricular activities, whether that's charging round a go-kart track, playing a spot of tennis or pretending to be a doctor and dispensing multicoloured pills in a *Tetris*-like setting. This time round, it's thwacking away at a tiny white ball in *Mario Golf*. The game features ten playable characters, four courses, and Tournament, Strike and Practice modes. There are also loads of variants when it comes to selecting your clubs and lining up your various shots out on the course.

As well as being a surprisingly in-depth sports sim with a Mario flavour, it also boasts some great RPG-style elements. If you choose not to opt for one of the ten characters, you can create your own and access lots of fun challenges as you walk around the courses. Even if you've never shown an interest in golf before now, this game is guaranteed to have you obsessing over your putts, drives and bogeys in no time.

Don't fancy playing as Mario? Tee off as 'Kid' instead.

Mario lines up to take his shot...

90

WAYS TO PLAY TODAY

RETRO RATING 4/5

Nintendo Switch Online
It's still not made its way on yet, but the N64 version of *Mario Golf* is scheduled to be released on Switch Online in the near future. And don't forget that patience is an essential golfing skill.

RETRO RATING 3/5

Nintendo 3DS
3D graphics and updated gameplay?! *Mario Golf World Tour* for the 3DS has it all when it comes to strolling across the virtual fairways.

? The Game Boy Color version of *Mario Golf* was released around the same time as it was on the N64. It included a nifty feature where you could plug your Game Boy into the console and transfer over various characters.

91

GAME BOY COLOR GAMES

METAL GEAR SOLID

WHAT'S IT ALL ABOUT?

It's time to be quiet. Very quiet. And almost invisible. Why? Because we're entering Solid Snake's world, where crashing about the place with an enormo-weapon is out and sneaking around corners and lurking in shadows is very much in.

Life's a stressful old business at the best of times, doubly so when your livelihood consists of super-intense, deadly stealth missions, which is why we find Solid Snake in retirement out in the wilds of Alaska. But as is so often the case, a quick round of gentle coaxing (with a dollop of guilt) is all it takes for him to tool up and get ready to take down a bunch of guerrillas (just to clarify, these are the evil terrorist variety, not the hairy banana enthusiasts) who've stolen a new version of the Metal Gear nuclear weapon platform.

The game takes a top-down view of the action; well, we say 'action' but rather than going in all guns blazing you've got to get your sneak on and use those shadowy nooks and crannies to make your way through each uber-tense mission. And tense they most definitely are. We guarantee you'll soon be absorbed in the pressurised atmosphere that will have you sweating as a guard approaches your hidey place and flinching with panic when they eventually spot you and all hell breaks loose. Sneak this into your game collection now.

Stay quiet and pick your moment carefully, or the guard will be on you!

WAYS TO PLAY TODAY

Nintendo 3DS

Unsurprisingly, as game hardware got more powerful Solid Snake's missions got more violent, which is why *Metal Gear Solid: Snake Eater* was saddled with an 18 rating despite being released on the 3DS.

? Completing the game opens up a whole wealth of extra stealthy content, including 180 bite-sized training missions to really hone your sneaky moves.

DONKEY KONG COUNTRY

WHAT'S IT ALL ABOUT?

You can't spend your whole life raging on top of a scaffold or charging round a go-kart track with Italian tradesmen; sometimes you just need to get back to nature. Which is exactly what our Donkey Kong has done…

In a way, *Donkey Kong Country* is about reversals of fortune. Our favourite monkey is no longer the villain and is happily living in his jungle world with his famous name passed safely on to his grandson. But the Kongs get a cruel taste of their own simian medicine when there are darn dirty apes led by King K Rool take diabolical liberties by stealing their banana hoard. The younger Donkey Kong and his even younger nephew Diddy Kong are out to take them back!

The Kong lads work as a team, with certain sections of the platform world requiring Donkey's strength and more ferocious attack moves and some demanding a little more finesse that suits Diddy's speed and superior jumping ability. You'll also meet the extended Kong family (Cranky, Funky and Candy) along the journey who help out in their own unique ways. The levels feel fresh and totally original, with a great variety of action that swings from swimming to mine-cart chasing to barrel blasting and, well, swinging. Plus they're all packed with small fun details and hidden nooks to discover. Who needs the Mario Brothers when you've got the Kongs?

No one gets away with stealing Donkey Kong's bananas!

WAYS TO PLAY TODAY

RETRO RATING 5/5

Nintendo 3DS
If you have a 3DS and few quid spare then the original game is yours to buy in all its simian glory, as this is an absolutely perfect version of the SNES classic that was ported to the Game Boy Color (if that makes sense!).

Super Nintendo Classic Edition
Not as easily available, but if you can track down a SNES reissue then you can play through Donkey and Diddy's banana-based adventure in the way it was originally intended: with a funky controller on a whacking great TV screen.

RETRO RATING 4/5

RETRO RATING 5/5

Nintendo Switch
You really are spoiled for choice when it comes to *Donkey Kong Country*, because you can also find it nestled among the classic SNES games that can be beamed straight to your Switch.

?

Donkey Kong Country started out as a boxing game! The title swiftly became the platforms-in-the-jungle concept we see here, but Kong's boxing skills were revived on the Wii where he was an unlockable character in an updated version of *Punch-Out!!*

GAME BOY COLOR GAMES

RAYMAN

❗ WHAT'S IT ALL ABOUT?

Another day, another platform franchise. But if you ever find yourself growing weary of the leaping-and-collecting shenanigans then this game is guaranteed to reignite the platform flame!

Rayman sees the titular hero setting out to free magical creatures known as Electoons who have been cruelly locked up in cages by evil Mr Dark and strewn around Ray's home world, which has been turned into a right old chaotic place in the process.

The gameplay is as you'd expect (ie super-fun leaping) and is set in a vibrant and constantly entertaining environment. Rayman himself starts out with fairly basic jumping and punching moves but can pick up new abilities on the way, some of which are temporary and specific to certain levels. You also need to pay close attention to your surroundings, as clearing some levels relies on you tracking down and triggering hidden switches, which is a neat touch that adds an extra element to the action. Even though he may be one of the lesser-known platform stars, Rayman (the character and the game) is well worth your time.

Look out for Tings to collect – find enough and you gain an extra life!

Rayman's world is about as bright and joyful as you can get!

WAYS TO PLAY TODAY

RETRO RATING 4/5

iOS and Android
If you prefer your platform fun to be mobile device-based, then head to your most convenient app store, download *Rayman Adventures* and get to work rescuing the Incrediballs!

RETRO RATING 5/5

Nintendo Switch, Xbox One and PlayStation 4
If you want to get a more up-to-date Rayman adventure then *Rayman Legends* is the one for you, featuring a top-notch quest and all the classic *Rayman* fun you've come to expect.

? In the early days the main character of the game was a young chap named Jimmy, who got sucked into his computer, turned into Rayman, and was tasked with taking on Mr Dark.

N64 GAMES

STAR WARS EPISODE 1: RACER

WHAT'S IT ALL ABOUT?

Thrills! Spills! No Jar-Jar Binks! This is *The Phantom Menace* spin-off game you are looking for. Get ready to pit your racing wits against the ultimate hive of scum and villainy.

Although it was a notorious cinematic clunker, *The Phantom Menace* did have a couple of redeeming features – Darth Maul and the pod race. And it's the latter that we have in game form here (but if any designers out there want to do an 'Adventure of Darth Maul' game, we're more than ready to take control of the red-faced Sith lord). The pod race was a fast and furious affair, filled with close racing action and suitably grubby tech. The game does a superb job of bringing this to your console with a healthy dollop of danger chucked in for good measure.

There are numerous characters that you can take control of and guide through the championship to win cash, upgrade your pod and achieve ultimate racing glory. The tracks are brilliantly designed and often a challenge to navigate at high speed – even without the added pressure of other pod-ers trying to knock you off course! If racing isn't your thing and you prefer pure pod piloting, there's also a Time Trial mode to test your skills against. The Force is strong in this one.

All the pods featured in the movie are available to race in the game.

WAYS TO PLAY TODAY

RETRO RATING 5/5

Nintendo Switch Online

Like many N64 faves, *Star Episode 1: Racer* is available to buy in all its glory from Switch Online. It also features a nifty motion-control update so that you are able to operate the twin pod engines individually.

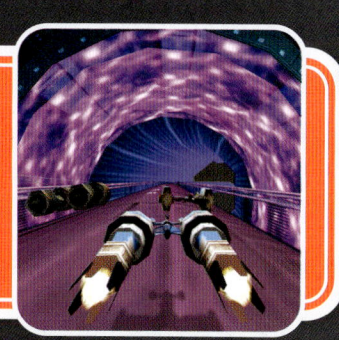

PlayStation 4

You can also get your pod-racing fix on the PS4. And although it doesn't feature the motion controls of the Switch (boo!), it does provide you with some suitable vibrations via the DualShock 4 pad (yay!).

RETRO RATING 3/5

> The game was originally titled 'Podracer' but had to drop the first three letters due to another company owning the rights to games with 'pod' in the title.

N64 GAMES

THE LEGEND OF ZELDA: THE OCARINA OF TIME

WHAT'S IT ALL ABOUT?

Another day, another adventure for everyone's favourite forest-dwelling elf. This time it's the Great Deku Tree that's in need of Link's services to defeat the evil sorcerer Ganondorf and his plans to enter the Sacred Realms and get his grubby mitts on the Triforce…

To be fair, this isn't just another adventure. It's a vast, epic adventure with side quests galore, puzzle-solving a-go-go and more combat than you can shake an elven sword at. There's also the ocarina itself – a handy object that has different uses depending on the songs that Link learns and plays. And learn and play it you must, as it's (unsurprisingly) essential to your quest. All of this spins out from the familiarity of the field of Hyrule, a beautiful and atmospheric landscape that Link has to carefully explore in order to reveal his goals.

The controls are as intuitive as ever, with Link's usual sword-slashing fighting technique spiced up with a variety of other weapons and an ace targeting system. The game is also perfectly paced, with the scale of the landscape never leading to you wearily trudging around searching for your next quest. Quite the opposite – it's a constant joy that never gets old. Grab your ocarina and get adventuring!

There are plenty of characters to help you on your quest. Although this doesn't look like good news!

WAYS TO PLAY TODAY

RETRO RATING 5/5

Nintendo Switch Online
As it's generally regarded as one of the best games ever, it's no surprise that *Ocarina* has had its fair share of rereleases. First up was a spin on the GameCube, followed by a turn on the 3DS, before settling in its new home as part of the N64 classics on Switch Online.

RETRO RATING 5/5

Nintendo 3DS
You may have noticed we mention the 3DS above, and as luck would have it, you can still access Link's musical odyssey via the Nintendo eshop and explore Hyrule in three glorious dimensions.

? When you reach Hyrule Castle Town and run into Malon for the first time, have a close look at her brooch — it resembles a Bowser head!

101

N64 GAMES

SUPER MARIO 64

WHAT'S IT ALL ABOUT?

It's quite literally time for a new perspective on an old classic, as the Mushroom Kingdom goes 3D and the multitalented plumber leaps back into action with a familiar adventure in a brand-new landscape.

There are two stages you usually go through when firing up a new Mario. First, eye-rolling weariness when you read that once again the story revolves around rescuing Princess Peach from Bowser, and then pure elation when you realise just how spectacularly awesome it is to play. Although the main story here may be overly familiar, the way you navigate it is brand-spanking new. Mario turns up at the Princess's castle for afternoon tea only to find out that ol' Bowsey has used the castle's 120 Power Stars to hold its residents hostage. Our favourite plumber has to use the various paintings (which are really portals) to recover said stars and free everyone.

The big upgrade from the SNES version is the move to 3D. And what a move it is, with the classic feel of the platform-based japes perfectly updated to match the stunning new environments. And even when you complete all 15 humungous courses there's still more to conquer, as only thorough exploration and experimentation will lead to you recapturing every last Power Star. When it's as fun as this, we're happy to go on defeating Bowser's one evil scheme until the end of time.

64-bit Mario has loads of new moves to learn and master!

WAYS TO PLAY TODAY

RETRO RATING 5/5

Nintendo Switch Online

When Nintendo announced it was adding classic N64 games to Switch Online, only one game could have been top of the list — and it was. (If that was too subtle, we're talking about *Super Mario 64*.)

Luigi and Wario were originally planned to be a part of *Super Mario 64*, but in the end they didn't make the cut. However, they were included when the game was released on the Nintendo DS.

N64 GAMES

BANJO-KAZOOIE

WHAT'S IT ALL ABOUT?

Take a bird, a bear, a witch, a castle, musical notes, jigsaw pieces and the ability to steal beauty and what do you get? One of the most fun and bonkers platform games on the N64.

If you own a Nintendo console of any sort, it's fair to assume you're partial to the odd platform game (after all, there are loads of them). And *Banjo-Kazooie* certainly is odd, but in an endlessly fun way. Banjo is a bear and Kazooie is a bird, and they both reside on Spiral Mountain. As does Gruntilda, a witch who's fond of rhyming and is so jealous of Banjo's sister Tooty's good looks that she steals her beauty. Banjo and Kazooie have to battle through her castle by collecting musical notes to unlock the various doors, and scoop up various jigsaw pieces called 'jiggies' to unlock the various levels. Confused yet? Well don't be, as somehow this all makes perfect sense once you fire up the game and get into it.

The levels are a varied bunch, ranging from a winter wonderland to a swamp and a cemetery. And all are imaginatively designed and filled with Gruntilda's cronies.

The gameplay is the standard platform stuff of leaping and collecting and disposing of baddies in a variety of clever ways. There's also a host of items to help you through each level, such as caterpillars to feed giant eagles and eggs to chuck at anyone who gets in your way. And to top it off, the whole game is shot through with a constantly chucklesome sense of humour.

One plays a banjo and one plays a kazoo, can you guess who is who?

WAYS TO PLAY TODAY

RETRO RATING 5/5

Nintendo Switch Online
After lingering on the 'Upcoming Games' list for a while, both Banjo and Kazooie have made the leap to the awesome set of N64 games included in the Expansion Pack membership. Happy days!

RETRO RATING 4/5

Xbox One
If you have an Xbox One, you can nab a copy of *Banjo-Kazooie* from the online store. Naturally, it's been spruced up with improved graphics and sounds.

> The game was originally only going to feature Banjo but as his abilities were expanded, the developers figured it made more sense to give them to a separate character. Enter Kazooie!

N64 GAMES

LYLAT WARS

WHAT'S IT ALL ABOUT?

Like all good baddies, you can't keep Dr Andross down for long. And so it is in this *Star Fox* follow-up that the evil scientist and emperor of Venom has declared war on the Lylat System. And first up is the planet Corneria!

Evil geniuses never learn, do they? Give them a damn good thrashing and they slink away for a bit before coming back for more. Luckily, Fox McCloud and his team never tire of delivering said thrashings. *Lylat Wars* (or *Star Fox 64* if you're outside of Europe) is yet more frantic, bombastic air combat of the galactic variety, with the action spread out over 15 levels that take in a variety of settings with suitably inventive and devilishly-tricky-to-beat bosses to contend with. The levels are interconnected, which means you can take a number of different paths through each, and the path you take determines where you end up next.

The action also shifts between being an 'on rails' shooter where you're essentially flying 'into' the screen and view the Arwing craft from behind, and an All Range mode where you can move totally freely in an arena-style setting. All the battles have an epic feel to them that rams home the scale of the environment you're flying in. Plus, the natural-feeling movements of the craft really immerse you in the missions. These are also neatly broken up, with land- and underwater-based missions that see you behind the wheel of a Landmaster tank and a rather nifty Blue-Marine submarine. And if you don't fancy taking on the wars by yourself, there's a fab four-player mode on offer. Here's hoping Dr Andross comes back for a third go — we can't wait.

Your Arwing craft has unlimited laser bullets and a handful of Smart Bombs.

WAYS TO PLAY TODAY

RETRO RATING 5/5

Nintendo Switch Online
After putting in a brief appearance on the 3DS (in 3D, obvs), *Lylat Wars* has now taken up residence among the other N64 games that are ready for downloading to your Switch.

?

There was originally a *Star Fox* sequel planned for the SNES. But with the release of the PlayStation around the time the game was ready, it was starting to look a bit out of date. No matter! The N64 was just around the corner so around 60% of the game was sliced off and developed into *Lylat Wars*.

107

N64 GAMES

SUPER SMASH BROS

WHAT'S IT ALL ABOUT?

If you've ever fancied socking Link in the kisser, drop-kicking Donkey Kong, or wiping the moustache off Mario (or Luigi's) face while pretending to be Samus Aran or Fox McCloud, then your wish has been granted!

There aren't many Nintendo characters who haven't ventured out of their classic and familiar environments. Usually it's for some light recreation on the golf course or the tennis court or the go-kart track, but to have them face off and batter each other senseless? We'd never have believed it had this game not plopped into our N64. There are 12 iconic characters to choose from and you can either guide one through Tournament mode or take on up to three of your mates in a four-player ruckus.

Rather than fights ending in knockouts or ripping your opponent's head off *Mortal Kombat* style, *Smash Bros* takes more of a sumo approach, with the aim of each match-up to knock Jigglypuff or Pikachu or whichever poor unfortunate is on the receiving end of the combat platform the most times before the clock runs down.

There are a number of stages to fight on, all based on classic games, and there are special moves to master and various weapons to deploy. Although it sounds a tad violent, *Super Smash Bros* has a similar vibe to *Mario Kart* in that it's fun and healthy competition that's shot through with a wicked sense of humour. You're sure to have a thumping good time.

Mario or Luigi? Which brother will come out on top?

WAYS TO PLAY TODAY

RETRO RATING 5/5

Nintendo 3DS
If the 3DS is more your handheld jam, you can get your mitts on a (bone) cracking version of *Super Smash Bros*, and while it may not be 'Ultimate' it still has more characters and fight arenas than the N64 version.

RETRO RATING 4/5

Nintendo Switch
Although the original is yet to be added to the roster of N64 games for the Switch, you can still get your kicks (and punches) with *Super Smash Bros Ultimate*, which has more characters, more moves and, well, more everything!

> The mysterious Master Hand is the brains (or fingers?) behind the *Super Smash Bros* universe and is also the final boss you have to take on. Unsurprisingly he's quite handy at slapping, punching and flicking!

109

N64 GAMES

MARIO KART 64

WHAT'S IT ALL ABOUT?

Bigger! Better! Faster! More fun! Mario and his fellow speed demons are back on track with this follow-up to the original karting classic.

The updating of classic titles for each new console is a Nintendo tradition that we're fully behind, and none more so than in the case of *Mario Kart 64*. What could better that fab racer, you may ask? Well how about 3D tracks with dips, gaps and bumpy terrain? How about more power-ups and cool stuff to chuck at your competitors? How about a multiplayer mode that enables four of you to go head-to-head-to-head-to-head on the most epic racetracks ever? (You get all these things, by the way.)

At its heart the gameplay remains the same – choose a character, hop in your kart and work your way through Mario Grand Prix mode by taking the top spot at tracks that make up each of the cups. The familiar items to leave in your fellow racers' paths are now available in multiples, along with a number of new additions. There's also the Time Trial mode if shaving a few seconds off a track record is your thing. The main focus is pure fun though. And you'd be hard pushed to find a game that does this better, with graphics as vibrant, and action as frantic. The only disappointment is seeing that final chequered flag.

Mario prepares to overtake, or maybe take out, Luigi!

WAYS TO PLAY TODAY

RETRO RATING 5/5

Nintendo Switch Online
Of course *Mario Kart 64* is available on Switch Online! Just imagine the outcry if it wasn't?! Grab your Expansion Pack, invite your friends and get racing.

RETRO RATING 5/5

Nintendo Switch
While the N64 *Mario Kart* only had room for four players to take to the track at once, *Mario Kart 8 Deluxe* on the Switch allows eight racers to battle it out for the chequered flag!

RETRO RATING 5/5

Nintendo Switch
Mario Kart Live: Home Circuit is the latest version of this classic game. It literally brings the racing larks into your own home as you control an actual kart and pilot it around your room of choice with all manner of enhancements popping up on your Switch screen!

> During development the main character in *Mario Kart* was just 'a guy in overalls'. That was until the team realised how cool it would look if Mario and the gang were behind the wheels instead.

N64 GAMES

YOSHI'S STORY

WHAT'S IT ALL ABOUT?

In a gaming genre that's mainly about happiness and fun, this could very well be the happiest and the funnest, as Mario's dinosaur pal takes his turn on the platforms…

This is a game with happiness at its very core. Yoshi always was a jolly old soul and here we find out why. The inhabitants of Yoshi's Island (where *Yoshi's Story* is set) keep up their jollity levels with the help of the Super Happy Tree, so when it's nicked by doom-and-gloom merchant Baby Bowser (who also casts a spell turning the happy place into a pop-up storybook) you can see why it's vital it's returned. Luckily, six about-to-hatch eggs survive the casting of the spell and the fledgling Yoshis are eager to head off to BB's castle.

Once you've chosen your Yoshi, the fun really starts, and it is terrific waddling around the beautifully rendered levels and pulling off all the classic moves we know and love, particularly the little fluttering motion you can add on to each jump to extend your air time. It's definitely aimed at younger gamers who may struggle with the intricacies of Mario's adventures in the Mushroom Kingdom, but the lack of challenge is more than balanced out by the sheer joy and playfulness of the levels. And you can't argue with a game in which one of the main goals is to be happier.

On each level you have to collect 30 fruits (like this delicious apple) to advance.

WAYS TO PLAY TODAY

RETRO RATING 5/5

Nintendo Switch Online
Get ready to be happy, because the story of the littlest dino is part of the growing N64 collection that comes with taking out an Expansion Pack membership on the Switch.

RETRO RATING 4/5

Nintendo Switch
If you're after more Yoshi, you're in luck, because as well as his many guest appearances in games, he also has many of his own, the latest being *Yoshi's Crafted World*.

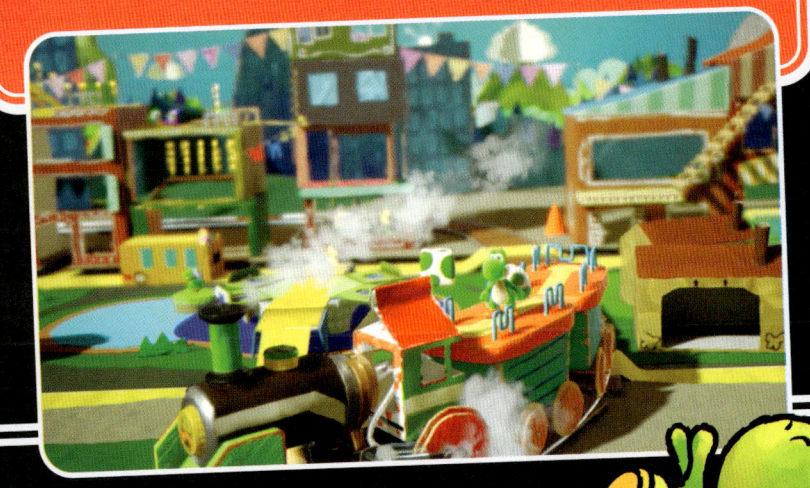

> Being a dinosaur, it stands to reason that Yoshi also has a fuller and slightly scientific-sounding name: T. Yoshisaur Munchakoopas.

N64 GAMES

STAR WARS: ROGUE SQUADRON

WHAT'S IT ALL ABOUT?

Another *Star Wars* game in our N64 round-up? You better believe it! And instead of hoofing it around planetary racetracks we're taking to the skies. The force is also strong in this one.

Released a long time ago and set in a galaxy far, far away, *Rogue Squadron* is an arcade-style combat game. It's set in the skies above various locations in the expanded *Star Wars* universe and takes place between the events of *A New Hope* and *The Empire Strikes Back* (films 1 and 2 or 4 and 5, depending on how you look at them, but that's a whole other argument!). Your job is to take control of Luke Skywalker himself and guide the Rogue Squadron to victory across 16 ace missions. There are classic aircraft to fly (which make intuitive use of the N64's analogue stick) and bonus ships to unlock as you battle your way through the Imperial forces.

Although the emphasis is placed on fast-paced arcade thrills, the game is fairly difficult to progress through. The controls and feel of the X-wings are easy enough to master but the missions themselves prove to be tough old things to conquer, and require many a fly-through to complete. That's not a bad thing, though, as the soundtrack and attention to detail in the graphics fully immerse you in the *Star Wars* universe to the point where you're totally happy to commit to multiple cracks at each mission.

WAYS TO PLAY TODAY

RETRO RATING 4/5

Nintendo Switch Online
Although *Rogue Squadron* is not available for the Switch, there are a number of equally good games that give the authentic *Star Wars* experience. Chief among them is *Jedi Academy*, where you learn the ways of the force from Master Luke.

Nintendo Switch
But if you're really only interested in piloting your way through a galaxy far, far away, fire up *Star Wars Squadrons* and then fire up a starfighter!

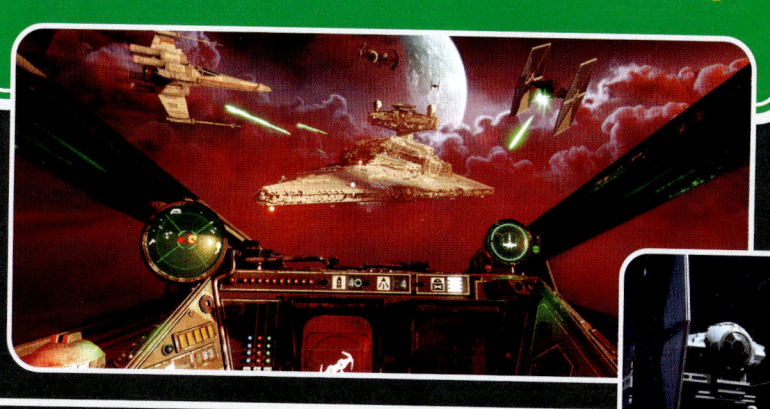

RETRO RATING 4/5

? *The Phantom Menace* was scheduled to be released after *Rogue Squadron* landed on the N64, and so a Naboo Starfighter was added to the game – the code to unlock it was revealed after the film hit cinemas worldwide.

N64 GAMES

TONY HAWK'S PRO SKATER 2

WHAT'S IT ALL ABOUT?

After a pretty good start, the Birdman's second outing sent the series kickflipping and McTwisting its way into the gaming stratosphere, taking the whole action sports genre with it.

The Tony Hawk games are great for many reasons – the authenticity, the soundtracks, the numerous real-life pros you get to control… But this has that magic that comes along all too rarely – it's super simple to pick up and incredibly difficult to put down. The premise is simple too! Pick a pro and guide them through various skate destinations (including some famous ones drawn from real life) and complete the requisite number of challenges to open up the next level. Outside of the Career mode there are multiplayer games, time trials and a level designer so you can create your dream park.

The control system is intuitive and does a fantastic job of creating the illusion of feeling like you're skating (largely thanks to the perfectly captured physics and sound effects). What really seals its reputation is the Free Skate mode, where you can take to the streets of any level you've opened and just skate. No time limits, no high scores, no challenges, just virtual skating at its finest. Grab your board and go skate!

Venice Beach is one of the many real-life locations for performing inventive combos.

WAYS TO PLAY TODAY

RETRO RATING 5/5

Nintendo Switch Online, PlayStation 4 and Xbox One
In 2020, the first two *Pro Skater* games got the next-gen HD treatment for a rerelease on numerous platforms in a single package with a 12 rating.

? The 900, Tony Hawk's signature special move in the game, took him 13 years to learn in real life. After landing his first one, he only did them occasionally because they were so hard and he announced he would (probably) never do one again after filming his last (or was it?) at the age of 48.

SEGA TIMELINE

Although it has faded from view in the games market of today, Sega still had a run that other companies could only dream of – pumping out awesome consoles and some of the best titles of all time!

Master System
With the 8-bit market booming, Sega brought out the Master System to take on the mighty NES.

1986

1983

SG-1000
Sega entered the console market in 1983 with this often-forgotten machine.

1988

Mega Drive/Genesis
Sega beat Nintendo out of the 16-bit gates with this mega-selling classic that boasted a legendary library of games.

CLICK, CLICK
1983 was quite the year – as not only was the computer mouse released onto the market, but the food boffins at McDonald's also invented the Chicken McNugget!

The Mega Drive was known as the Genesis in the US, due to a trademark dispute.

118

SSSNAKE

Even though it snuck in just as the decade was ending, the Nokia 3210 mobile phone became a bestseller. Partly because you could play the incredibly addictive *Snake* on it. And so began the trend of phones mainly being used for anything other than making calls!

Game Gear
What could be better than the Game Boy? How about a handheld gaming device in colour? Just don't mention the battery life...

Dreamcast
Another great console that sadly couldn't quite compete against the triple threat of the PlayStation 2, GameCube and Xbox.

1990

1998

1994

Saturn
This was a slight misfire! In spite of some worthy titles, the Saturn failed to set the world alight.

HATCHING TURTLES

The *Teenage Mutant Ninja Turtles* first burst out of the sewers during the 80s. They came about after artist Kevin Eastman sketched a turtle holding some nunchucks, and his friend Peter Laird wrote 'Teenage Mutant' next to it. The rest is reptile comic-book history!

MASTER SYSTEM GAMES

GHOULS 'N GHOSTS

WHAT'S IT ALL ABOUT?

Behold! The medieval-themed arcade classic that's probably most famous for having a main character who's forced to take on demonic minions while wearing only his pants!

More on the pants thing later. The story of *Ghouls 'n Ghosts* is a simple one: Sir Arthur's companion Princess Guinevere has been kidnapped by the Demon Emperor Sardius, and it's up to Arty to leg it through all manner of spooky locales (graveyards, ice caverns, sinking pirate ships — that sort of thing), dispatch as many shuffling and shambling types as he can, rescue Guinevere and get back home in time for tea (okay, maybe not that last part). There are various weapons on offer to lob, some more useful than others, and you have a suit of armour to keep you fit and healthy.

So, the armour. Whereas most games have an energy meter or some other way of measuring damage to the main character, in *Ghouls 'n Ghosts* your armour falls away when you get hit by an enemy projectile, leaving you to forge ahead wearing just your under-crackers. Whether intentionally or unintentionally hilarious it somehow fits with the tone of the game, which is simply relentless side-scrolling weapon-chucking action. It's also another of those notoriously difficult games, so be prepared for the long-haul. It's time worth investing, though, as it's an awesome experience.

One of the many undead baddies who's desperate to see you in just your pants!

WAYS TO PLAY TODAY

RETRO RATING 5/5

Nintendo 3DS and Super Nintendo Classic Edition

Both the handheld and the SNES reissue give you access to *Super Ghouls 'n Ghost*, which not only has better graphics but also gives Arthur the ability to 'double jump' (and yes, he's still in his undies).

RETRO RATING 4/5

Xbox One and PlayStation 4

Packaged along with the first instalment, *Ghouls 'n Ghosts Resurrection* has made its spooky way to the PS4 and Xbox with enhanced graphics (and pants) and the same insanely high difficulty level.

? If you manage to conquer all the levels, instead of being rewarded, you're informed that you've been tricked and must play them all again at a higher difficulty level to properly complete the game! The cheek of it!

SPEEDBALL 2: BRUTAL DELUXE

WHAT'S IT ALL ABOUT?

Future sports tend to be fairly anarchic affairs, and none more so than this combination of ice hockey and handball with added punching. It's time to limber up and get down and dirty!

Sports games rarely have plots, but this one does. It's the year 2105 and the once-banned sport of Speedball has experienced a big resurgence – in a more controlled yet more violent form. The Speedballers of old have been tempted out of retirement and Brutal Deluxe are the worst team in the league. It's up to you to make them the best.

The game is easy to understand – you score points by lobbing the ball into the opponent's goal and the highest score wins. There are various devices in the midfield that multiply the points if you chuck the ball through one first, plus there are recesses in the wall where you can gain an extra two points by lighting up a star. There are also no rules, so being handy at belting someone in the chops is just as vital as goalmouth action. This fast and furious game offers plenty of bone-crunching futuristic fun.

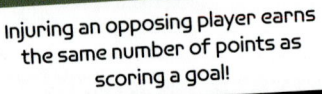

Injuring an opposing player earns the same number of points as scoring a goal!

When not in the arena, players can be trained up to boost their abilities.

WAYS TO PLAY TODAY

RETRO RATING 4/5

Steam
In 2013 *Speedball 2* was given a hi-def spruce up and made available for PC users via Steam. The original gameplay is present and correct along with a host of expanded features.

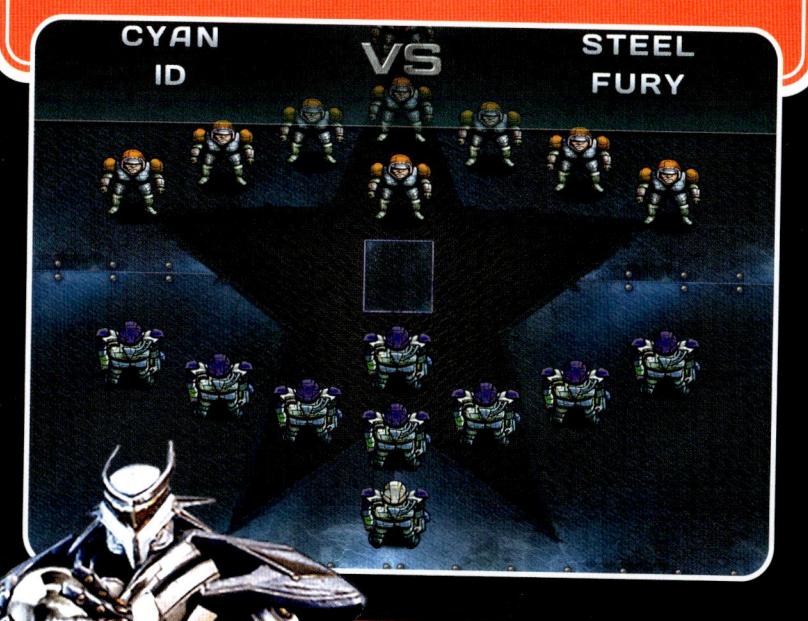

> The basic design of the game was worked out by the development team on a scrap of cardboard at a local pub. Just weeks later it was sold to a publisher and given the green light.

MASTER SYSTEM GAMES

CALIFORNIA GAMES

❗ WHAT'S IT ALL ABOUT?

If any game justifies breaking out the embarrassing dude-speak, it's this one. Ready? Here goes: it's, like, totally radical! Hang ten, bro!! Shred the gnar! (We're very, very sorry.)

Nowadays we have the X Games and all manner of board sports popping up in the Olympics, but way back when, the idea of a tournament featuring various action sports was quite the innovation. *California Games* brings together surfing, skateboarding, BMX and rollerskating with the lesser-known but popular-at-the-time disciplines of footbag and flying disc. The gameplay is simple: compete in each event, score the highest marks and bathe in the sun-drenched Californian glory.

In a way it's tricky to evaluate the action here as these sorts of games have moved on so much over the years and incorporated stunning levels of realism. But this is still a super-fun game nonetheless, and honing your skills and learning ever-more impressive tricks is incredibly absorbing and rewarding. Plus it looks great and does a good job of capturing the general vibe of these uber-cool pursuits.

A world of sun-kissed, palm-tinged sporting antics awaits...

Simply pull off as many tricks as you can without falling off (or going to the hospital).

WAYS TO PLAY TODAY

RETRO RATING 4/5

Nintendo Switch, Xbox One and PlayStation 4

After putting in a brief appearance on the Wii, *California Games* has rather faded from view. But if you're in need of an action sports fix you can't go far wrong with the *Tony Hawk* series.

> *California Games* has a number of quirky extras, such as being able to hit a seagull during games of footbag, sometimes enduring an earthquake during the skateboarding event, and getting abducted by a UFO if your flying disc skills aren't up to scratch.

MASTER SYSTEM GAMES

AFTER BURNER

WHAT'S IT ALL ABOUT?

Get ready, because we're about to fly right into the danger zone in one of the most thrilling air-to-air combat games to ever land on an arcade cabinet or home console!

Nowadays you'd be hard-pushed to find a game without a story and at least one main character, but that wasn't always the case. *After Burner* ditches any sort of narrative and throws you straight into the action. And what crazy action it is! Your missions (should you choose to accept them) are to fly your F-14 Tomcat through 18 stages, destroying any and all enemy jets that wander into your crosshairs with chonking great machine guns and heat-seeking missiles.

As you can probably imagine, the gameplay is unrelenting. Enemy planes attack from all sides meaning you have to be just as handy with your reflexes and barrel rolls as you do with targeting and deploying your weapons. Strategy plays a big part too, as launching a heat-seeker results in a big plume of smoke that momentarily obscures your vision — time it wrong and you won't see the fatal shot coming your way. Although there's not a massive amount of variety in the missions, it really doesn't matter, as the basic action and the excitement of being at the controls of a seriously tooled-up fighter jet is strong enough to carry this game on its own.

After Burner was popular enough to gain a stonking sequel with even more flying-and-shooting mayhem!

WAYS TO PLAY TODAY

RETRO RATING 4/5

Nintendo 3DS
An enhanced version was released for the 3DS in the form of *3D After Burner 2*, a remastered version of the classic with added levels, modes and numerous gameplay enhancements.

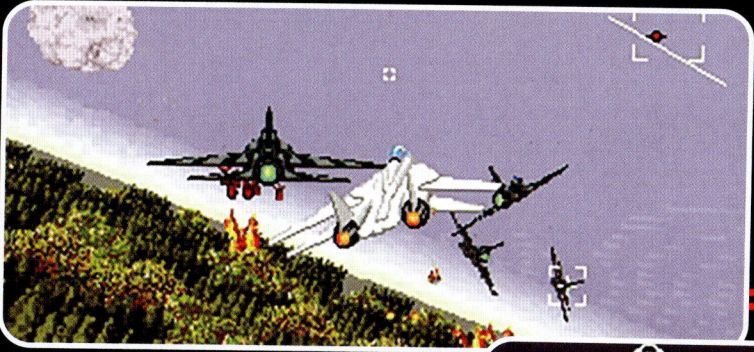

? This is a game that's well worth tracking down in its arcade form, as one version features a sit-in cockpit that rotates and tilts for the full immersive experience (minus the bullets and missiles, obviously).

MASTER SYSTEM GAMES

ALEX KIDD IN MIRACLE WORLD

WHAT'S IT ALL ABOUT?

While all the attention was focused on Mario and his platform pals, another gaming superstar was quietly doing his thing over on the Master System. Say hello to Alex, the gaming icon you've probably never heard of...

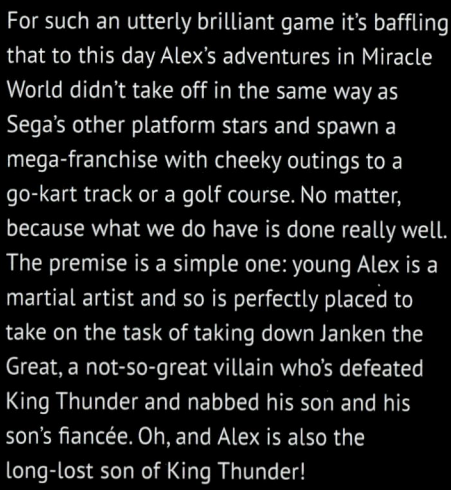

For such an utterly brilliant game it's baffling that to this day Alex's adventures in Miracle World didn't take off in the same way as Sega's other platform stars and spawn a mega-franchise with cheeky outings to a go-kart track or a golf course. No matter, because what we do have is done really well. The premise is a simple one: young Alex is a martial artist and so is perfectly placed to take on the task of taking down Janken the Great, a not-so-great villain who's defeated King Thunder and nabbed his son and his son's fiancée. Oh, and Alex is also the long-lost son of King Thunder!

The levels are of the usual high standard you'd expect from a platform classic, and Alex is equipped with a tasty punch that can vanquish enemies and break rocks to open up new paths. The game shifts between side-scrolling levels and single-screen ones, which provides great pace and variety. It also has a rather curious inclusion: at the end of a number of levels the boss battle consists of a game of rock-paper-scissors. It's odd because a large element of chance is introduced into completing a level. But do you know what? We kind of like it. And we love the rest of the game too!

Smashing rocks can also reveal handy items such as bags of money.

WAYS TO PLAY TODAY

RETRO RATING 4/5

Nintendo Switch
If you fancy playing the original, you're more than welcome, as the *Sega Ages* collection includes Alex's classic platform caper.

RETRO RATING 4/5

Nintendo Switch, PlayStation 4, Xbox One and PC
Get ready for a real treat, as *Alex Kidd* has also had a long-awaited remake. *Alex Kidd in Miracle World DX* is a stunning reboot featuring gorgeous graphics, new levels and ultra-fun gameplay.

Back in the day you didn't need to shell out your hard-earned cash on a separate cartridge to take a crack at Alex's adventures because it came built into the Master System!

MASTER SYSTEM GAMES

ASTERIX

WHAT'S IT ALL ABOUT?

We're back to classic cartoon-y platform territory. In this case, it's 55 BC and the residents of a certain Gaulish village are still causing the Roman armies no end of bother...

If you're not familiar with the comics, Asterix and Obelix are residents of the last village in Gaul not to be overrun by the Romans. The reason for that? The magic potion their druid Getafix brews that gives them and their fellow villagers super-human strength. The game is very much based around the basics of the comics and sees Getafix getting kidnapped and taken to Rome, leaving Asterix and Obelix no option but to fight their way through the Roman legions and rescue him using their last reserves of potion.

The game settles on a satisfying mix of platforming dexterity and puzzle-solving ability as you dispatch unfortunate Roman soldiers with the 'paffs' and 'thwoks' of the Gaulish haymakers loved by comic fans. This is the highpoint of the game, as the graphics perfectly capture the look and feel of the characters and do a great job of putting you in their world. You can play as both Asterix and Obelix – once you complete a level as one you get to play it again as the other with the features tailored to that character.

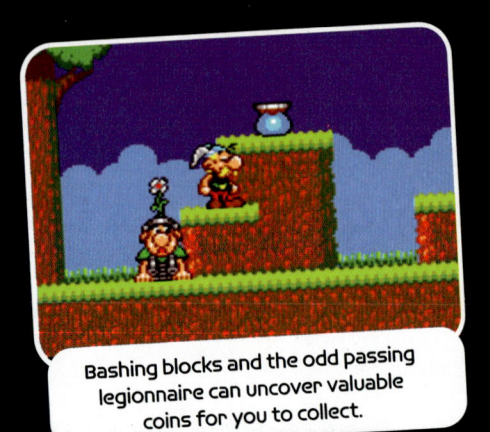

Bashing blocks and the odd passing legionnaire can uncover valuable coins for you to collect.

Try as they might, the Romans simply can't take control of Asterix and Obelix's village.

WAYS TO PLAY TODAY

RETRO RATING 4/5

iOS and Android
If you prefer more of a role-playing approach over platform-based capers for your Gaul-ish fun, we highly recommend downloading *Asterix & Friends*, where you can build your own village before going off adventuring.

Nintendo Switch, PlayStation 4 and Xbox One
Although the Master System version is unavailable as a reissue, there are loads of other *Asterix* games to get your mitts on. *Asterix & Obelix XXL 2* has a similar Getafix-rescuing plot, and for authentic Roman-biffing you should take a look at *Asterix & Obelix: Slap Them All!*

RETRO RATING 5/5

> The mega-successful *Asterix* comic books are published worldwide and have been translated into around 100 languages. There are also 40 video games, 15 board games, 18 films and one theme park.

MASTER SYSTEM GAMES

THE NEWZEALAND STORY

WHAT'S IT ALL ABOUT?

It's more platform japes ahoy! And this time we're off to the far side of the world to help out the NZ wildlife and jump off a load of stuff in a variety of settings. (PS We actually love this type of game!)

After vacuuming up any and all spare change in the arcade world, *The NewZealand Story* eventually landed on the Master System, where it ruffled feathers with its own peculiar brand of platform-based cuteness and addictive gameplay. You take control of Tiki, a kiwi who's out to rescue his girlfriend Phee Phee and a bunch of her mates from a blue leopard seal who's been causing some aggro in the land of sheep farming and near-unbeatable rugby players. (Disclaimer: those last two things may not be mentioned in the game.)

Don't let the cuteness fool you as Tiki is tooled up with a bow and arrow and whatever else he finds lying around – he has no problem commandeering a balloon or other flying machine by booting out its unfortunate occupant. The levels take no prisoners either, and include some fiendish mazes, baffling puzzles and combat that often requires cunning and super-quick reflexes. There really is nothing like *The NewZealand Story*, and it's this baffling combination of cuteness, action and humour that keeps you glued to what can be some pretty challenging levels. There's also a part where Tiki rides on the back of a laser-spitting duck – now who can say no to that?!

WAYS TO PLAY TODAY

RETRO RATING 4/5

Nintendo DS
The New Zealand Story Revolution popped up on the DS back in 2007 – an ace remake that made good use of the DS tech. There's a good chance of tracking down a copy – a secondhand DS and the odd cartridge or two aren't that hard to come by.

? The game was inspired by one of the programmers taking a trip to New Zealand. Judging by what's included in the finished version, it must have been one heck of a holiday!

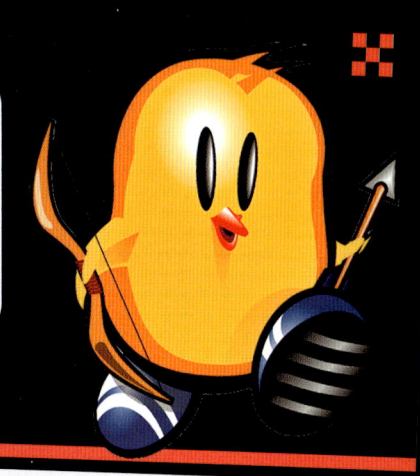

MASTER SYSTEM GAMES

EARTHWORM JIM

❗ WHAT'S IT ALL ABOUT?

We've had foxes, hedgehogs and turtles, so why not worms? Prepare to get down and dirty with one of the most unique characters and games in the retro canon...

You may think that a slow-moving invertebrate would be an odd choice for a nimble platform game and it seems the developers may have done too, which is why the plot is centred on Jim (the earthworm) happening upon a special suit that gives him the ability to move about like a human and defeat Queen-Slug-For-a-Butt, who wants the suit so she can kidnap Princess What's-Her-Name.

As you can probably tell, *Earthworm Jim* has a unique sense of humour, and this runs through the game like a cheeky word through a stick of rock. End-of-level bosses include the magnificently named Professor Monkey-For-a-Head and Bob the Killer Goldfish, and one level involves a bungee-jumping contest against an opponent made of snot. And talking of levels, there's fantastic variety, taking in wickedly fun and funny platform affairs, racing challenges and riding a hamster through underwater tunnels. There are few games that stand out as much as *Earthworm Jim* and you owe it to yourself to play this game.

Hanging by his head while shooting baddies – just a normal day for Jim.

WAYS TO PLAY TODAY

RETRO RATING 5/5

Mega Drive Mini
The essential Mega Drive Mini contains the 16-bit version of *Earthworm Jim* in all his glory, complete with the bonkers sense of humour that made him a star back in the day.

RETRO RATING 4/5

Steam
All three *Earthworm Jim* games (the original, the sequel and the HD remake) are available to download via Steam to your desktop or laptop, and all are well worth seeking out.

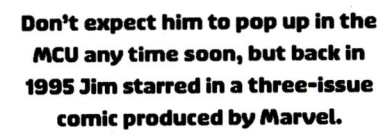

? Don't expect him to pop up in the MCU any time soon, but back in 1995 Jim starred in a three-issue comic produced by Marvel.

MASTER SYSTEM GAMES

R-TYPE

WHAT'S IT ALL ABOUT?

Yawn, this is just another shoot 'em-up, right? Wrong! There may be the usual hordes of dastardly aliens to blast to kingdom come, but *R-Type* brings its own style and swagger to the space-blasting genre.

R-Type is anything but 'just another' shoot 'em-up, and is packed to the galactic gills with space-related thrills and extraterrestrial spills. The game sees you take on the Bydo Empire, a race of aliens who, as is so often the case, have massed on the edge of the galaxy and are preparing to invade Earth, and only you can give them a damn good stuffing!

A huge amount of work has been put into the sci-fi graphics, and levels and aliens alike simply ooze with space grime. The gameplay is top-notch too – strategy and positioning are the order of the day rather than simply mashing the buttons and causing all manner of destruction. Your ship can be kitted out with power-ups and laser-blasting gizmos, all of which are vital to strafing a path through the alien meanies and taking down the end-of-level bosses. It is truly out-of-this-world stuff!

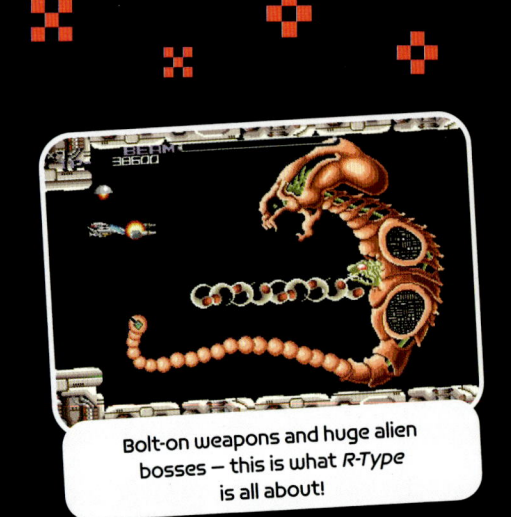

Bolt-on weapons and huge alien bosses – this is what *R-Type* is all about!

Modern-day *R-Type* is a force to be reckoned with, as are the all-new alien beasties!

WAYS TO PLAY TODAY

RETRO RATING 4/5

Nintendo Switch, PlayStation 4 and Xbox One

Not only can you get a 3D version of the original *R-Type*, it also comes bundled with its equally ace sequel, *R-Type Dimensions*. All the original levels are present and correct, along with a handful of new modes.

Nintendo Switch, PlayStation and Xbox One

If you want to get bang up to date (and get more bang for your buck), the latest version of *R-Type* is where it's at. *R-Type Final 2* has more levels, more weapons and more aliens.

RETRO RATING 4/5

One of the weapons you can bolt onto your ship is a glowing orange ball known as the 'Force'. Among the programmers it was known as 'the dung beetle'.

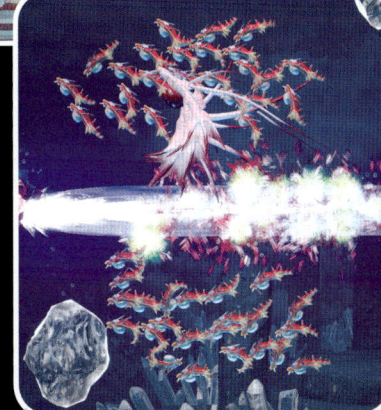

MASTER SYSTEM GAMES

GAUNTLET

WHAT'S IT ALL ABOUT?

It's time to go underground to discover just what lurks in those dank, dark dungeons. And it's no surprise to learn that it's a load of beasties that are out to do us in. We wouldn't have it any other way!

In *Gauntlet,* you (and an optional friend) choose to play as either Thor the Warrior, Merlin the Wizard, Thyra the Valkyrie or Questor the Elf and are dropped into a dungeon maze to fight your way through hundreds of evil ghouls, ghosts and other assorted monsters to find the exit. Then you do it all over again in another, even more fiendishly designed dungeon, where you'll face even more fiendish creatures and demons.

There's a splash of puzzle-solving and route-finding involved in the game, but really it's action all the way. And it's played at a tremendous speed too, with hordes of the undead swarming on you at once as you try and hack and slash your way out, sometimes sheer panic. Each of the characters has their own abilities and strengths and so you need to choose wisely if you're teaming up in two-player mode. But that's really where the strategy ends, as this is the very definition of a turn-off-your-brain-and-mash-those-buttons title.

Cooperating with your fellow mythical player is vital to seeing off the swarms of baddies.

Meaner and moodier – the updated *Gauntlet* is a gory supernatural slash 'em-up.

WAYS TO PLAY TODAY

RETRO RATING 3/5

Xbox One

The superb *Midway Arcade Origins* collection features a ghoulish dungeon's worth of classic games, including not only the amazing *Gauntlet* but its devilish sequel as well! If you're over 16, you can get it on the Xbox One via the online store.

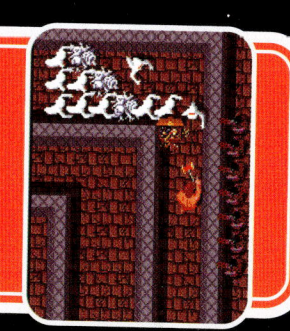

PlayStation 4

RETRO RATING 4/5

Gauntlet was revived for the PlayStation 4 as *Gauntlet: Slayer Edition*, but unfortunately the vastly gorier graphics and gameplay landed it with a 16 rating. The original was rereleased as part of *Midway Arcade Treasures* and can still be tracked down for PlayStation 2, Xbox and GameCube (but only if you're in your teens).

> In case the dungeons and the wizard and the elf didn't give it away, *Gauntlet* was inspired by the legendary game *Dungeons & Dragons*, which we can't recommend enough if you fancy some non-console-based gaming.

GAME GEAR GAMES

BUBBLE BOBBLE

WHAT'S IT ALL ABOUT?

It's toil and trouble time as you take control of bubble-spewing dinosaurs and fight your way out of screen after screen of super-fun platform japes!

Poor old Bub and Bob. One minute they're minding their own business, the next they've been turned into bubble-blowing dinosaurs by Baron Von Blubba and have to fight their way through 100 levels of bubble-based bonkers-ness in the Cave of Monsters. The Baron's baddies can be captured in bubbles and then butted into oblivion as the buddies barge their way Baron-wards.

As well as being fond of the letter 'B' (and who isn't?!), the game is an absolute delight to play. It's essentially a platform affair but with the action on each level restricted to a single screen. Although this means that you don't have the same scope for exploration as you'd find in other titles, the focus on a single problem gives the game a fast pace that's quite welcome. Naturally the levels get tougher and the baddies more ingenious as you progress, but the difficulty is well judged and you won't find yourself stuck on a particular level for too long – there are various power-ups to gobble for a bit of a boost. Maybe being transformed into a bubble-dino isn't so bad after all… ?

Blow a bubble to trap an enemy and then burst it to get rid of them. Easy!

WAYS TO PLAY TODAY

RETRO RATING 5/5

Nintendo Classic Mini
If you prefer to see Bub and Bob in their authentic retro setting, you can get your fix on the NES Classic Mini.

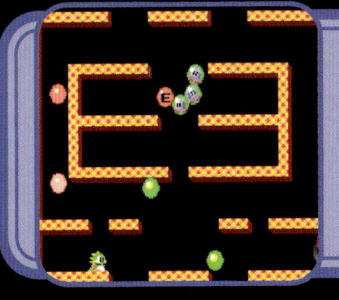

RETRO RATING 3/5

iOS and Android
The classic bubbly platformer has been shrunk down and made available for some on-the-go bubble-dino action.

RETRO RATING 5/5

Steam, Nintendo Switch and PlayStation 4
Bubble Bobble 4 Friends is a terrific update, with new levels, strategies and multiplayer modes. And best of all, it also comes packaged with the original!

? One of the main motivations game designer Fukio Mitsuji had for producing *Bubble Bobble* was that he just liked the idea of filling the screen with bubbles and then popping them. Which is fair enough.

GAME GEAR GAMES

SPACE HARRIER

WHAT'S IT ALL ABOUT?

Like a lot of Master System shoot 'em ups, this ditches the lengthy backstories, launching headlong into a brightly coloured world full of deadly delights that need a good laser-ing!

Dragons – they're a tough bunch, right? Scaley, handy with the old fire-breathing and able to swoop from the sky – you'd think they could take care of themselves. Well, not when a load of mutated aliens are after them and want to take over their fluorescent checkerboard world known as the Fantasy Zone. So who's going to help them? How about a bloke called Harrier clinging on to the side of a jet-propelled laser blaster? Yes, he'll do nicely.

And that's *Space Harrier* in a nutshell. You take to the skies and blast seven shades out of whatever beastie comes screaming towards you, which also include evil robots and the occasional mammoth. What the game lacks in storyline it makes up for in action, which is impressively fast and requires lightning-quick control-pad skills. It's mega-challenging too, with a fair bit of practice needed to make it to and past each of the bosses that lurk at the end of every level. If you're after a no-nonsense shooter with added dragons, look no further.

The key to conquering each level is to never stop moving (or firing).

WAYS TO PLAY TODAY

RETRO RATING 5/5

Nintendo Switch
The *Sega Ages* collection is doing a terrific job of keeping the Sega flame burning, and this ace version of *Space Harrier* is very much a part of it.

RETRO RATING 3/5

iOS and Android
Although the original isn't available, you can get your hands on the mega sequel, the aptly named *Space Harrier II*, which features new weapons and a whole load of new aliens to blast!

RETRO RATING 4/5

Mega Drive Mini
If you've played through the original and are keen for more clinging-on-to-a-laser-blaster action, the 16-bit sequel *Space Harrier II* is part of the Mega Drive Mini collection.

? Much like *After Burner*, the arcade version of *Space Harrier* also features a hydraulic chair that attempts to mimic the movements you make on screen. Alas, there were never any hydraulic dragons to go with it.

GAME GEAR GAMES

DR ROBOTNIK'S MEAN BEAN MACHINE

WHAT'S IT ALL ABOUT?

Not content with his hedgehog-bothering antics, Sonic's arch nemesis has turned his attentions to creating an army of robot slaves via the medium of a colourful *Tetris*-style game...

The poor bean people of Mobius just didn't see it coming. They were all minding their own business when a notorious villain from another franchise turned up and decided that turning them into a robot army would be a nice way to spend the afternoon. And the method? His Mean Bean-Steaming Machine. Luckily, plucky bean person Has-Bean is on hand to put a stop to this.

The plot doesn't tell you much about the game mechanics, which are incredibly simple. Pairs of coloured beans simply drop into your column, and you have to move and rotate them to create horizontal or vertical rows of four. Once you've done that they disappear leaving more room for more beans. It differs from Tetris in that you go head-to-head with a series of 13 opponents. The more four-bean lines you create, the more beans get chucked into your foe's column – fill their column and you've won. Perfect your bean-matching with Puzzle mode, where you have to get rid of certain sets of beans, and Exercise mode where you can practise the main game. Much like its block-based Russian counterpart, this is hopelessly addictive to play and a real challenge to master.

Creating chain matches causes unmatchable grey beans to drop into your opponent's column! Mwahahahaha!

144

WAYS TO PLAY TODAY

RETRO RATING 4/5

Mega Drive Mini
Although the Game Gear version is out of reach, you can play the 16-bit upgrade via the Mega Drive Mini and manipulate beans to your heart's content.

RETRO RATING 4/5

Nintendo Switch Online
If you prefer your beans to be handheld (so to speak), Switch Online has you covered (not literally) thanks to the evil doctor putting in an appearance on the ever-reliable Sega Expansion Pack.

Mean Bean Machine is based on a mega-popular Japanese game called *Puyo Puyo*. Rather than beans, it revolves around matching tiles and is just as tough to put down!

GAME GEAR GAMES

THE GG SHINOBI

WHAT'S IT ALL ABOUT?

Watch out, there's ninjas about! Grab your sword and get ready to stealthily cut a swathe through the latest bunch of unfortunates to get in Joe Mushashi's way. And this time they've also come for his mates…

If you thought ninjas were more of the lone wolf type, don't worry… we did too! But in *Shinobi* world they come in gangs, and poor old Joe Mushashi's chums have been put under a spell by the evil Zeed crime syndicate that's turned them against the forces of good — and their bezzie mate, Joe! He's having none of it, though, and is out to save both them and the day by thumping the Zeed very hard indeed.

Shinobi is a top-notch beat 'em-up that mixes side-scrolling combat with the one-on-one variety in the form of end-of-level bosses. The various levels provide a great mix of action, with Joe leaping from car to car on a highway, clinging on to a cliff face in a treacherous valley, shimmying up trees in a forest, and dealing with a harbour-side Zeed base. Every aspect is exciting and challenging and is backed up by some brilliant animation and suitably bone-crunching sound effects.

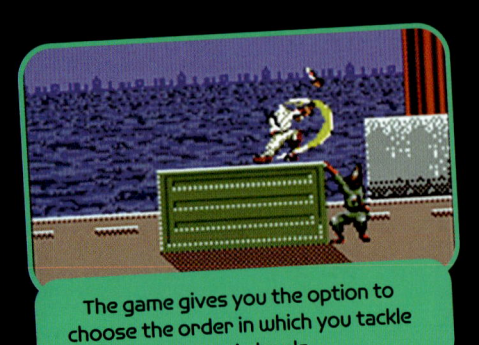

The game gives you the option to choose the order in which you tackle the main levels.

Once you've rescued a ninja pal you have the choice to play as them instead of old Joe.

WAYS TO PLAY TODAY

RETRO RATING 4/5

Xbox One and PlayStation 4
The GG Shinobi was adapted for the 3DS Virtual Console back in 2013 but it's no longer available. However, the 12-rated *Sega Mega Drive Classics* features *Shinobi III: Return of the Ninja Master*.

RETRO RATING 4/5

iOS and Android
While you can no longer get *The GG Shinobi*, *The Revenge of Shinobi Classic* is available to download from the Apple App and Google Play stores. However, *The Revenge of Shinobi Classic* is available in app form.

RETRO RATING 4/5

Nintendo Switch
Sega Ages is an ever-expanding roster of games that have been converted to the Switch. And as luck would have it, the original *Shinobi* is one of the games available in the series.

? Scattered throughout the game are boxes Joe can crack open to access power-ups. Just be careful what you hack at, as some contain bombs, which don't have quite the same nourishing effect.

GAME GEAR GAMES

OUTRUN

WHAT'S IT ALL ABOUT?

You have to be fast but it's definitely not a time to be furious in this sedate-yet-swift tour of some dead-classy European highways and byways.

Head-to-head racing is great, but sometimes it's nice to just enjoy the car and the scenery, which is where *OutRun* comes in. Set across 15 stages inspired by picturesque European settings (we're talking Swiss Alps and the Mediterranean here, the M25 and its ilk unsurprisingly don't get so much as a look in), the goal is simply to complete each course in your super-sleek and super-swift Ferrari Testarossa Spider within the time limit while avoiding daily traffic.

The different roads present their own unique challenges, and the game is tough at times, but the emphasis is on sitting back and enjoying the ride rather than worrying about what hordes of rabid petrolheads are up to in your rearview mirrors. The controls are as easy and smooth as you'd expect for a game of this style and there's a great soundtrack to bring the scenery to life that you can control on the in-car radio. Simply turn on, tune in and drive out.

OutRun introduces you to the genuinely simple pleasure of calmly overtaking a lorry.

In-car DJs can select their own bangin' tunes!

WAYS TO PLAY TODAY

RETRO RATING 4/5

Nintendo Switch Online

In 2019 *Out Run* (various versions are spelled as either *Out Run* or *OutRun* – don't ask us why…) cruised onto the Switch. And rather than being a modern update, it was the classic version that you could find on the Game Gear.

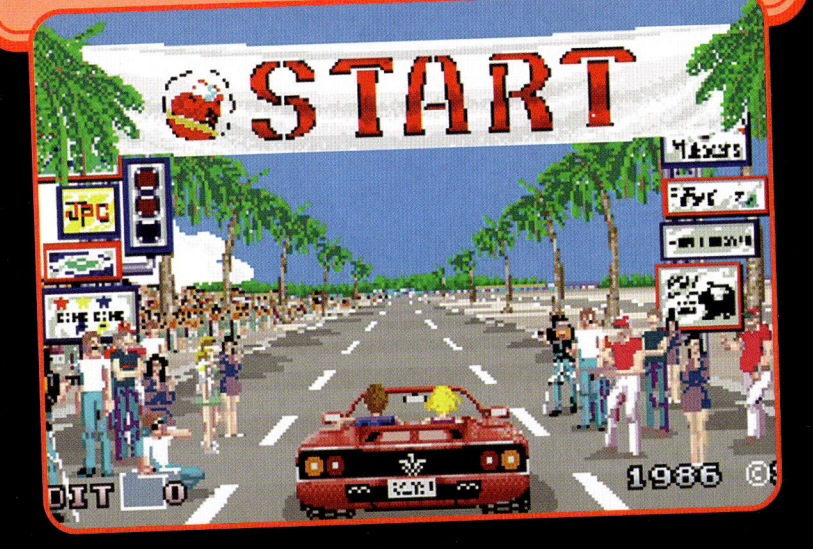

OutRun designer Yu Suzuki also came up with arcade classic *Hang-On*, where you sit astride a model bike. He originally wanted to put a real engine in it for an 'authentic' feel but had to settle for a bass-heavy speaker instead. No prizes for guessing why…

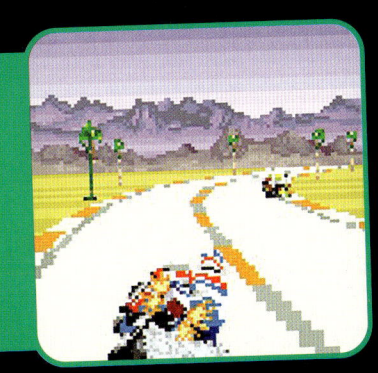

MEGA DRIVE GAMES

STREET FIGHTER II

WHAT'S IT ALL ABOUT?

They're fighting! In the streets! Again! Welcome to the knuckle-crunching, bone-rattling world of *Street Fighter II* – the absolute undisputed world champion of console beat 'em ups. Are you ready?

It's simple – choose a fighter, square off against another fighter, and when you've done that, take a breather before dishing out the same treatment to the remaining warriors. Once you've made your way around the world and through your seven fellow competitors, it's time to face the final four lads who prequalified for the tournament on account of being legendary hard cases.

As always there's more to it than that. Each fighter, from martial arts master Ryu to fire-breathing Dhalsim, has their own special moves and styles that need to be understood and mastered, whether you're playing as them or fighting against them. The basics need work too, as the three levels of punch and kick on offer mean that weaker ones can be dished out swiftly but the more damaging strikes are slower to execute and leave your guard down. Mix this massive variety of fighting techniques, combos and strategy in with brilliantly detailed backgrounds and a thumping soundtrack and you have a fighting sim that is hard to beat.

Ryu delivers a tiger uppercut to Sagat, one of the four final bosses.

WAYS TO PLAY TODAY

RETRO RATING 5/5

Nintendo Switch, Xbox One and PlayStation 4

Street Fighter 30th Anniversary popped up on the major consoles back in 2018, but is now saddled with a 12 rating (age ratings weren't a thing back in the early 90s). We guarantee it's worth the wait, though!

RETRO RATING 5/5

Nintendo Switch

Ultra Street Fighter II: The Final Challengers. It's the *Street Fighter* we know and love but better! More play modes, more characters and gorgeous manga-style graphics.

The game was named after a Japanese movie called *Clash, Killer Fist!* that was renamed *The Street Fighter* in America. After the game became a hit, it was itself turned into a movie that made a fair amount of cash, but only has a 10% rating on film website Rotten Tomatoes.

151

MEGA DRIVE GAMES

SONIC THE HEDGEHOG 2

WHAT'S IT ALL ABOUT?

The blue spiky hero takes to the platforms with his fox buddy by his side to save the world once again. Strap in because although it's not a bumpy ride, it is most definitely a super-sonic one!

Dr Robotnik just loves a bit of world domination, and Sonic similarly loves halting world domination — they're a match made in hedgehog heaven. This time around, the bad Doctor's new scheme is to seize control of the Chaos Emeralds with his army of robots and use them to power his brand-new space station, the Death Egg (an homage to *Star Wars*' Death Star... although we should point out it's the developers' homage, not Dr Robotnik's). Sonic's not alone in his battle as he has his new and trusty sidekick, Tails the Fox, to help him barrel through West Side Island and thwart the evil genius's wicked plans.

Sonic is all about speed and spectacular action, and there's plenty of that on offer as you leg it through the twists, turns, loops and springboards of each level, collecting rings as you go. There's also a series of stunning bonus stages where the game shifts into a 3D perspective as Sonic and Tails barrel down a pipe. All the worlds are wonderfully detailed with many different routes through each one that are all well worth discovering. And the occasional bit of cooperative play with Tails adds an extra dimension to the platform fun. Get hold of a copy, fast.

Play as Sonic or Tails or both. Or select two-player mode and grab a mate to control Tails (or Sonic).

152

WAYS TO PLAY TODAY

RETRO RATING 4/5

iOS and Android
Sonic the Hedgehog 2 is available on mobile along with a host of other hedgehog-related spin-offs. Our only gripe is that the ads are a tad intrusive. But it's free, so hey-ho!

RETRO RATING 5/5

Nintendo Switch Online
Along with its own back catalogue, Nintendo has also made a number of Mega Drive classics available on Switch, including old bluey's outing that you see here.

RETRO RATING 4/5

Xbox One
Sonic and Tails also put in an appearance on the Xbox 360, which has now been carried over for download onto your Xbox One in all its classic glory.

Tails' full name is Miles Prower, which is a play on 'miles per hour'. If you didn't spot this immediately, don't worry — it took us, ooooh, about 30 years to realise.

MEGA DRIVE GAMES

DISNEY'S ALADDIN

WHAT'S IT ALL ABOUT?

An awesome platform game without an Italian plumber or a blue hedgehog or other miscellaneous cute animals? Well, there had to be at least one, didn't there? And what a game it is…

When you think of Mega Drive platformers you go to *Sonic* and then pretty much lose track. Which is a shame because *Aladdin* is every bit as good as the blue hedgehog's speedy battles with Dr Robotnik. Mostly following the plot of the Disney flick of the same name, *Aladdin* sees you take control of Aladdin himself and set out to rescue love-of-his-life Jasmine from the up-to-no-good Grand Vizier Jafar. The epic quest takes in the Agrabah Markets and rooftops, the Cave of Wonders and the Sultan's Dungeon (among many other locations) before ending with a showdown at Jafar's palace.

The platform and action gameplay is epic, with superb animation and sound blended with incredibly satisfying level design to put you right in the classic animated movie. Rather than simply leaping and punching, *Aladdin* has a scimitar to slash at his enemies along with apples to lob at them. There's a good mix of action too, with magic-carpet riding sitting seamlessly alongside rope climbing and monkey-bar work. There are even super fun mini games thrown in for good measure. If you're ever granted three wishes, use one to get hold of this game!

Use the scimitar for close-up action, and the apples for long-range attacks.

Keep your eyes peeled for a handy magic carpet when navigating this level.

WAYS TO PLAY TODAY

RETRO RATING 5/5

Nintendo Switch, PlayStation 4 and Xbox One

The *Disney Classic Games Collection* is an absolute must-buy, as not only do you get the version of *Aladdin* you see here, you also get all the versions released for other consoles, plus the *Lion King* (below) and *Jungle Book* games!

Be sure to watch out for the many subtle nods to other Disney classics, such as some Mickey Mouse ears on a clothesline and Sebastian from *The Little Mermaid* in the Palace Dungeon!

155

MEGA DRIVE GAMES

MORTAL KOMBAT

❗ WHAT'S IT ALL ABOUT?

Surely no one-on-one fighting game could be tough enough to square up to the colossal might of *Street Fighter II*, right?! Wrong! There was one that accepted that very challenge, and square up it most certainly did...

There are a few things that are familiar about *Mortal Kombat* if you're a seasoned fight enthusiast. For starters, there's a selection of characters with different moves and abilities, and each fight is a best-of-three affair staged as part of a tournament (in this case on Shang Tsung's Island). But rather than manga-style graphics, the game has opted for realistic-looking fighters with real-looking moves.

The action itself is more measured too, with the arcade thrills of *Street Fighter* dialled back and the emphasis placed just as much on blocking and counter-attacking as it is on flailing headlong in a whirl of haymakers and boots on the botty. Each fighter also has their own particular 'Fatality' move, which is basically a needlessly gory way to finish off an opponent. Plus there are a series of mini games called 'Test Your Might' where you bash the living daylights out of various inanimate objects (which is curiously satisfying). If you like your fighting games with a not-so-healthy spray of blood, sweat and tears, this is the tournament for you.

Liu Kang takes a kick to the noggin courtesy of Sub-Zero.

WAYS TO PLAY TODAY

RETRO RATING 3/5

Xbox One, Nintendo Switch and PlayStation 4

The original *Mortal Kombat* led to the introduction of game ratings, and so most (if not all) versions are now out of reach. The latest version, *Mortal Kombat 11*, unsurprisingly landed itself with an 18 rating. Sorry, kids!

By all accounts it was tough coming up with a title for this game! *Kumite, Dragon Attack, Death Blow,* and *Fatality* were all considered before the makers settled on *Mortal Kombat.*

MEGA DRIVE GAMES

STREETS OF RAGE 2

! WHAT'S IT ALL ABOUT?

If *Mortal Kombat* has a bit too much ick for your liking, the arcade-style thrills of this side-scrolling battle-fest could be just the thing.

In a still-unnamed city, Mr X has risen from the pasting he took in the first game to exact revenge on our intrepid brawling heroes. One of the gang has been kidnapped and Axel, Blaze, Skate and Max aren't going to rest until they've gotten him back via the time-honoured tradition of hitting bad guys jolly hard until they do what they're told.

Streets of Rage 2 is a blast. It's fast-paced, challenging, and has a combat system that's bursting with variety. All the fighters at your disposal have different skills, styles and unique 'blitz' attacks – all of which can be bolstered by grabbing various weapons that are scattered around the aggro-filled pavements. The main two-player mode is of the cooperative variety, and gives you the ability to pull off some seriously nifty combo moves. And if you're in a more antagonistic mood, there's a separate Duel mode where you can knock the stuffing out of your mates. Hit the streets and check this out now.

Not getting cornered is a pretty vital strategy for making it through each level!

Come on, Axel – what part of 'don't get cornered' did you not understand?!

WAYS TO PLAY TODAY

RETRO RATING 4/5

Nintendo Switch Online
The ever-trusty Switch gives you access to the original *Streets of Rage 2* via the Mega Drive games included in the Expansion Pack. And for those over 12 there's the latest version – *Streets of Rage 4*.

? *Streets of Rage* composer Yuzo Koshiro was influenced by Brit electronica bands such as The Orb and The Prodigy. The soundtrack is widely considered one of the best of all time!

MEGA DRIVE GAMES

ECCO THE DOLPHIN

WHAT'S IT ALL ABOUT?

And now for something complete different (again) with what is essentially a dolphin simulator. Bear with us, though, as this odd premise bloomed into a truly beautiful game...

If you're expecting an action game set in a large aquarium where you have to perform tricks for fish, you've assumed wrong! This is about exploring the wild blue ocean in a surprisingly involved adventure that's full of surprises and the occasional puzzle. As the title suggests, Ecco is a dolphin – a bottle-nosed dolphin to be precise. Ecco has to track down the other members of his pod after they're swept away by a mysterious hurricane. If that sounds a bit too real-world for you, don't worry, because the game eventually involves time travel and an ancient race of aliens.

Despite the sci-fi elements that pop up later on, this game is still a mostly tranquil experience (even if you do have to ram the occasional enemy at high speed), as you take control of Ecco and glide through the clear waters. Interaction with other marine life is accomplished through Ecco's ability to 'sing', which you can also use to map different areas via echolocation. Don't forget dolphins need the odd breath or two, so you have to factor in surfacing now and then to gulp down air. One feature that may divide opinion is that the tasks aren't obvious – you can spend a fair bit of time just bobbing about trying to figure out what to do next. But that's all part of this unique and compelling adventure.

There may be jellyfish knocking about, but this is still one of the most serene gaming moments ever.

WAYS TO PLAY TODAY

RETRO RATING 5/5

Mega Drive Mini
Like all games that have been bundled on to this pint-sized console, *Ecco the Dolphin* is reproduced perfectly and still plays like a dream.

RETRO RATING 5/5

Nintendo Switch Online
If the Switch is more your thing, you can get your flippers on Ecco by shelling out for the Expansion Pack that gives you access to the classic Mega Drive lineup.

Ecco almost ended up being named Botticelli due to the massive popularity of the Ninja Turtles! We're presuming that never extended to also making him a bit tasty with a set of nunchucks.

MEGA DRIVE GAMES

ANOTHER WORLD

WHAT'S IT ALL ABOUT?

Most platform games tend to be bright and cheery, but it's time for a change of pace as we get all moody and tense on a mysterious alien planet that's as hostile as it gets…

Science experiments can be tricky beasts. Take the case of Lester Knight Chaykin, for example. All he wanted to do was spend the evening in his lab, accelerating some particles and pondering the birth of the universe — the usual stuff. But then, BANG! Lightning strikes and a hole in space and time opens up, transporting the poor lad to a hostile alien planet. What rotten luck. However, it's the start of a wonderfully intriguing and atmospheric platform action-adventure, so it's not all bad.

The platform action is squarely in the *Prince of Persia* camp and requires you to take a more measured approach to the terrain. Problem solving is key and there is often a lot of trial and error involved when it comes to conquering the gaps in front of you. The action picks up later in the game when Lester acquires a laser pistol but the emphasis is still on the almost parkour-style moves you need to make in order to explore the seriously atmospheric surroundings. And this leads us on to the animation, which is simply superb – it's hard to believe this was done in the days before motion capture. This is a journey to the stars that is well worth taking.

One of the many super-atmospheric levels to explore on your adventure.

WAYS TO PLAY TODAY

RETRO RATING 4/5

Xbox One, Nintendo Switch and PlayStation 4

Another World is available on the Switch with the original gameplay firmly intact and nicely augmented with remastered graphics and sounds. But as is sometimes the case with reissued games, it's now subject to a 12 rating.

? Another World creator Éric Chahi took a unique approach to setting out the gameplay. Rather than planning ahead, he preferred to improvise 'without knowing where it was going'.

MEGA DRIVE GAMES

TOEJAM AND EARL

WHAT'S IT ALL ABOUT?

Aliens get a pretty bad rep in console games. Most of the time they're portrayed as an angry bunch who are just out for some intergalactic aggro. Not these two lads – they're more than happy to just go for a cheeky stroll...

Meet ToeJam and Earl – ace rappers and (below-average) spaceship pilots from the planet Funkatron. So below average that they've managed to crash their spaceship on Earth and now need to find all ten pieces (it was clearly a very precise crash) along with their megawatt speakers. Standing in their way are the increasingly eccentric residents, who have left some helpful presents but are mainly there to get in our new pals' way.

You'd be hard pushed to find a game as dedicated to laughs as this. The goal of the game is almost secondary to the pure enjoyment of wandering about, dodging jet-packed Santas, hypnotic hula dancers, lovelorn cherubs, trident-wielding comedy devils, and many more weird and wonderful inhabitants. The presents are a hoot to collect too, as although some are useful (spring shoes, munchies or Icarus wings, for example), another might contain a deadly storm of tomato rain! The two-player mode is great too, with the rappers going their own ways in a split-screen arrangement and high-fiving each other when they cross paths. Not just the best alien rapper game you'll play, but one of the most unique games ever.

Play as ToeJam or Earl, or grab a mate and control them both simultaneously!

WAYS TO PLAY TODAY

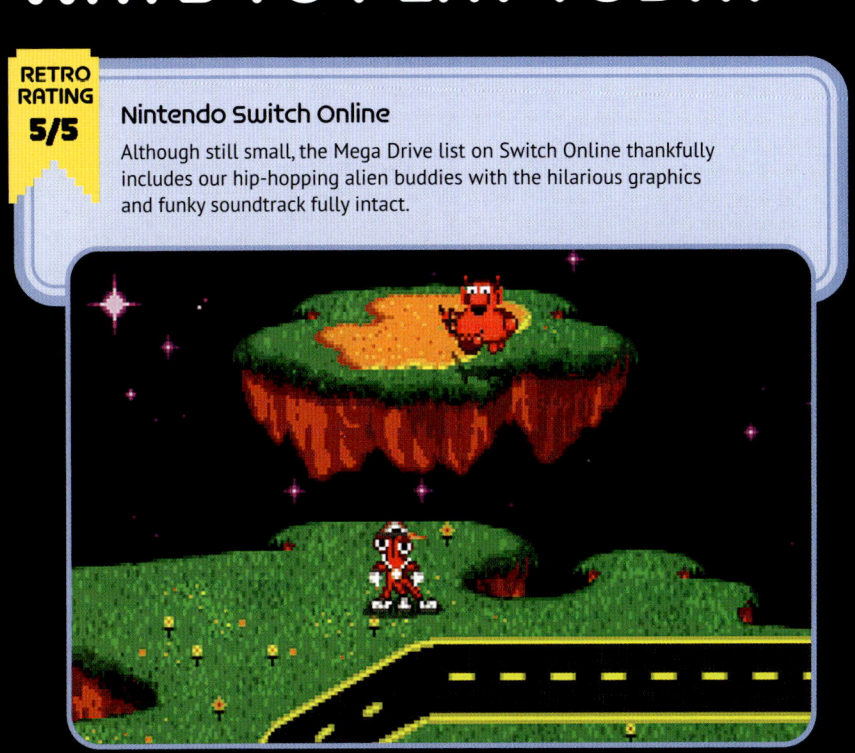

RETRO RATING 5/5

Nintendo Switch Online
Although still small, the Mega Drive list on Switch Online thankfully includes our hip-hopping alien buddies with the hilarious graphics and funky soundtrack fully intact.

ToeJam and Earl were originally called FlowJam and Whirl, but a programmer misheard and entered the names as we know them today. Sega liked them and so the 'wrong' names remained.

MEGA DRIVE GAMES

RISTAR

WHAT'S IT ALL ABOUT?

The star of this mid-90s platform caper is literally a star! And with big old stretchy arms to boot. Perfect for taking on an evil space pirate...

If you've not heard of *Ristar* before, blame the Sega Saturn. The Mega Drive was nearing the end of its life and Sega's notorious 32-bit flop was still being anticipated as a great leap forward, hence not many people wanted to spend their cash on a new game when they could save for a new console, no matter how good the game was. And *Ristar* is very, very good. The action takes place in a side-scrolling platform environment where space pirate Kaiser Greedy has used mind control to take over the leaders of various planets in a galaxy far, far away. And *Ristar*? He's out to stop him!

The big feature of *Ristar*'s gameplay is its hero's and multipurpose stretchy arms. Ristar can grab enemies from a distance and, pinging towards them, destroy them with a monstrous headbutt. He can also use the same motion for cracking open treasure chests. His arms can move in eight directions, enabling him to reach areas that he otherwise couldn't with his rather feeble jumps. As you can imagine the possibilities of this mechanic are vast and need to be deployed creatively throughout the game, making it vital that you master it. This was the last great game of Sega's 16-bit era and is still an essential addition to your collection.

As well as head-butting enemies Ristar can use his stretchy arms to swing on them!

WAYS TO PLAY TODAY

RETRO RATING 5/5

Mega Drive Mini
Even though it was largely ignored at the time, *Ristar* has seen something of a renaissance in the retro rerelease era, and is now part of the roster on the Mega Drive Mini.

RETRO RATING 5/5

Nintendo Switch Online
The *Ristar* reappraisal also extends to the handheld scene, where it can be found among the list of games that Switch users can access via the Expansion Pack.

RETRO RATING 4/5

iOS and Android
And let's not forget the mobile device in you pocket, to which you can also download the antics of everyone's favourite stretchy-armed celestial body.

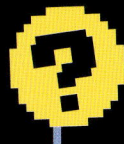

? In the early days of development, the main character was set to have long rabbit-like ears that could pick up objects, but it was eventually decided that arms would be easier.

MEGA DRIVE GAMES

TAZ-MANIA

WHAT'S IT ALL ABOUT?

Take a spin through the land down under with our favourite Tasmanian resident and discover exactly what's lurking in the lost valley (spoiler alert – it's not what you think...)

Nipping out for eggs may not sound like a great premise to base a game around, but *Taz-Mania* uses it to create one of the most enjoyable platform games on the Mega Drive. It all starts with Taz hearing about giant flying reptiles that, legend has it, can produce eggs that could feed a family of Tasmanian Devils for a whole year! Hungry chap that he is, he decides to head out and bag himself a few! It's up to you to guide him to them.

Taz-Mania manages to liven up all of the usual things we expect from a platform game in a number of ways. First, there's the non-linear levels that require you to find your way through rather than just keep running right while leaping. Second, there's a stronger puzzle element than on many other Mega Drive platformers. And third, there's Taz himself! He is never not entertaining as he navigates the endlessly fun world in his own particular way. This is about as faithful to the classic cartoons as you can get. Truly egg-cellent stuff.

Taz can eat most things he comes across, and scoffing these chillies gives him the ability to breathe fire!

WAYS TO PLAY TODAY

RETRO RATING 3/5

Xbox One
Alas, *Taz-Mania* is not available in any updated form and the Taz games rather fizzled out – his last appearance was *Galactic Taz Ball* on the DS. However, you can catch up with some of the other Looney Tunes gang in *Space Jam: A New Legacy – The Game*.

RETRO RATING 3/5

iOS and Android
But if jamming in space isn't your thing, you can find the Looney Tunes on iOS and Android in the rather nifty action-RPG, *Looney Tunes World of Mayhem*, which also features our Taz.

? Taz is a rather restless little chap and if you leave him standing in one place for too long he starts to get very annoyed indeed!

CHARACTER QUIZ

Which classic video-game character are you most like?
Choose from the answers below to find out!

1
Have you ever played golf in your spare time?
a. Only when my go-kart's knackered.
b. I have no time for such trivial nonsense.
c. It's a bit slow for me.
d. I think I'd prefer galloping across the fairway in search of a new side-quest.

2
Do you like collecting rings?
a. Nah, I'm more of a coin man.
b. Unless it's a space ring that has a bounty on it I'm not interested.
c. It's all I live for!
d. Only if they're magic. And play music.

3
What type of world would you prefer to knock around in?
a. Brightly coloured and named after an edible fungus.
b. Hostile, alien and filled with deadly organisms.
c. Anywhere with lots of springs to bounce off.
d. Mainly lush and green with a smattering of naughty warlocks.

4
What would you do if you had to hunt a version of yourself made from a space parasite?
a. Make my excuses and go back to my day job as a plumber.
b. Chase it!
c. Run away!
d. Assume I'd somehow wandered into the wrong game.

5
Do you like running really fast while being followed by a fox who doesn't really do much?
a. What do you think I am? A blue hedgehog?!
b. No, I'd probably get annoyed and shoot it.
c. Sounds like a plan!
d. It's one of the few things I've never done on a quest.

6
Are you interested in racing go-karts?
a. Yes!
b. No!
c. They're not fast enough for me.
d. Depends – can I drive it into a dungeon?

7

What type of nemesis would you prefer to face off against?
a. One with a spiky shell.
b. Any sort of space pirate.
c. A doctor (preferably evil) with a luxurious 'tache.
d. Whoever's won over a princess this week.

8

Do you often find yourself in poorly lit dungeons?
a. Of course I do! I'm an iconic platform character!
b. Only space dungeons.
c. Yes, but not as often as some people (elves, for example).
d. *Sigh* More often than I'd care to mention.

9

Do you like mucking about in subterranean worlds?
a. Only if they're accessible via a vertical pipe.
b. It's what I live for!
c. Yes, but only if a two-tailed fox can come with me.
d. If it's partially lit with flaming torches, I'm in.

10

What would you do if a talking tree asked you to go on a heroic quest?
a. Just shrug – it's certainly not the oddest thing that's happened to me.
b. Shoot it.
c. Run at it in the hope it contained some rings.
d. Saddle up a horse and get adventuring!

RESULTS

MOSTLY AS: You are **Mario!** Despite famously being a plumber there's very little evidence you've ever fixed a toilet.

MOSTLY BS: You are **Samus Aran**! You never go anywhere without a powered exo-skeleton. (Unless it's been surgically removed due to being infected with space parasites.)

MOSTLY CS: You are **Sonic**! You like living in bushes, sleeping in unlit bonfires and eating cat food... Sorry, that's an actual hedgehog!

MOSTLY DS: You are **Link**! You'll do anything if it's framed as a quest, and love to accessorise your outfits with a sword and rustic shield.

DREAMCAST GAMES

SONIC ADVENTURE

WHAT'S IT ALL ABOUT?

He's back! He's faster! He's in 3D! And he's brought more of his mates this time, which is all the better for frustrating the ever-evil Doctor Robotnik, who's bent on causing all manner of chaos.

Each Sonic game seems to introduce more of the hedgehog's pals. Back in number two we had Tails and now you can play one of six characters, with Knuckles the Echidna, Amy Rose, Big the Cat and E-102 Gamma joining the party – sorry, adventure! And what an adventure it is, with the gang out to take down Doctor Robotnik and his robot army who are after the seven chaos emeralds and the ultimate evil-doer himself, Chaos.

As well as the usual super-sonic action we all know and love, *Sonic Adventure* comes with an added splash of role-playing and a hefty sprinkle of non-linear gameplay. The levels are all accessed from various Adventure Fields and each of the six characters has specific skills they need to use once there. For example, E-102 is a dab hand with a laser blaster, while Amy Rose is a stealthy puzzle solver. This all combines to add shifts to the style and pace of the gameplay that is unfamiliar in other *Sonic* titles, but very welcome. And there's also all the mini game fun you could ever want. Yet another standout title in a classic series.

There are plenty of new features, but legging it as fast as you can is still at the heart of Sonic's adventures.

WAYS TO PLAY TODAY

RETRO RATING 4/5

Xbox One
Sonic Adventure was given a reboot for the Xbox 360, and jolly good it is too. Head over to the Xbox Live store to download it for your Xbox One.

RETRO RATING 4/5

Nintendo Switch
The latest super-fast-paced hedgehog-based adventure is *Sonic Colours Ultimate* on the Switch, which is stunning to look at and mind-meltingly fast, as you'd expect.

? The development team wanted a realistic feel to the levels and so visited South America to check out some ancient ruins and stroll through the jungles.

DREAMCAST GAMES

SEGA BASS FISHING

WHAT'S IT ALL ABOUT?

And now for something completely different – fishing. On a console. We're taking a trip to the wonderful world of competitive bass fishing!

Now this is a bold idea! And not only did that boldness take in the game itself, it also extended to the release of the Sega Fishing Controller to give that authentic feel of casting and reeling in a big ol' bass. The core of the game is a timed competition, in which you have to land a certain weight of fish before the timer runs down. There are different types of lures to use to entice the slippery prey onto your hooks, and you also need to be canny about where you cast your line. There are four stages to compete in at different times of the day, and then it's on to the final in a one-fish-takes-all cast off.

So is this game a bit gimmicky? Not a bit of it! It's packed with strategy as you test out different lures and get a feel for the various weather conditions, lakes and times of day. And using the fishing rod controller really helps to immerse you in your environment.

It's also surprisingly fast-paced, with the countdown timer adding some arcade-style thrills. Give it a try and you'll be hooked from the first cast.

One of the many bass (who may or may not be called Big Mouth Billy) that you have to hook.

WAYS TO PLAY TODAY

RETRO RATING 4/5

Xbox One
Although you can't get hold of the fishing rod controller, the usual control pad works just fine for this downloadable version of the Xbox 360 version of Sega's fishy classic.

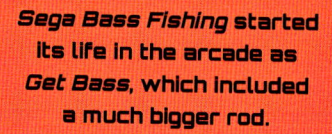

Sega Bass Fishing started its life in the arcade as *Get Bass*, which included a much bigger rod.

175

DREAMCAST GAMES

METROPOLIS STREET RACER

WHAT'S IT ALL ABOUT?

Forget go-karts, forget lobbing stuff at your mates, and forget hurtling about like a wazzock – this is where racing gets serious. But don't let that put you off – it's still heaps of fun!

'Serious' is probably the wrong word – how about 'realistic'? Yes, that works nicely. *Metropolis Street Racer* involves more thrills and spills than you can shake a gear stick at, but there's a fair bit of emphasis on impressing your fellow racers with your style and control. *MSR* features a whopping 262 tracks that are made up of blocked-off streets in recreated cities around the world. The various challenges (including Fastest Lap, Street Race and One-on-One) are presented in sets of ten, with the completion of each set opening up the next and also gaining you a new and snazzier car.

Make no mistake, this game is a tough wheel nut to crack. But that's fair enough when realism is the order of the day and gaining the necessary level of souped-up car mastery is so immensely satisfying and absorbing that you won't notice the hours tick by. The tracks are brilliantly designed and thought out too, and the cities are impressively recreated for this pre-Google Earth time. This is one game you won't regret getting behind the wheel of.

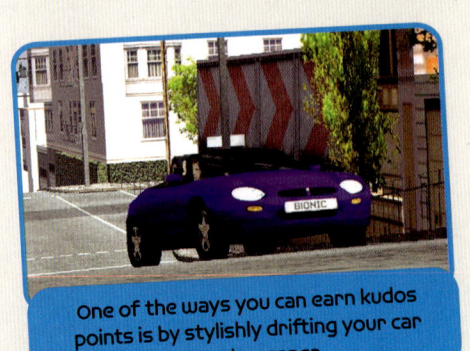

One of the ways you can earn kudos points is by stylishly drifting your car round a corner.

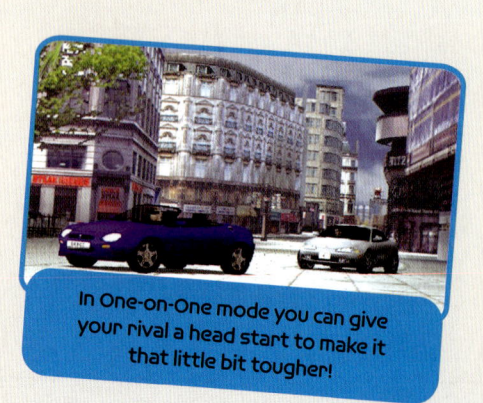

In One-on-One mode you can give your rival a head start to make it that little bit tougher!

WAYS TO PLAY TODAY

RETRO RATING 3/5

SEGA Dreamcast
Metropolis Street Racer was released on the Dreamcast and the Dreamcast only. There are no other consoles and rereleases, which is a real shame as it's sooooo good. You'll just have to keep an eye out on the secondhand market…

? Although it's quite a common thing now, *MSR* was the first game to feature in-game radio stations with DJ bants between the tracks.

VIRTUA TENNIS

WHAT'S IT ALL ABOUT?

If you ignore the slightly baffling scoring system, then tennis is a wonderfully simple game to get to grips with. As is its awesome virtual cousin that we see here in front of us today…

Knocking a ball back and forth has been popular with gamers ever since *Pong* bounced onto screens way back when. But *Virtua Tennis* really knocks it out of the court with a superb recreation that sees you take control of a player and face off against the big names of the day in various five-match tournaments. All the different playing surfaces are present and correct with the ball reacting differently on each, and every player has their own strengths and weaknesses, giving you a good excuse to play each tournament multiple times.

Virtua Tennis started life in the arcades, so naturally it has a control system that's easy to learn, with slices, lobs, smashes and all manner of other racket-based malarkey immediately on hand. There's a good deal of strategy involved as positioning and anticipating what your opponent might choose to do next are key to conquering the tournaments and climbing up the world rankings. Throw in a handful of super-fun training sessions that are more like mini games and you have the best tennis sim ever.

Each of the players have their own strengths and weaknesses to adjust to.

WAYS TO PLAY TODAY

RETRO RATING 4/5

iOS and Android

Head over to your favourite (and compatible) app store and you'll find *Virtua Tennis Challenge* – a fab update that's been tailored for mobile devices.

? If you'd invested in the fishing rod controller for your bass fishing odyssey, you were in luck, as it was also compatible with *Virtua Tennis!*

DREAMCAST GAMES

CHUCHU ROCKET!

❗ WHAT'S IT ALL ABOUT?

If you're thinking that the Dreamcast sounds like a fairly serious and grown-up console, fear not. It also has its very own brand of supreme bonkers-ness in the form of this mice-and-cats-and-rockets puzzle game!

Set in a space port (that looks suspiciously like an expanded chess board), *ChuChu Rocket!* follows an unfortunate race of mice (the ChuChus of the title) who find their cosy home invaded by a load of cats known as KapuKapus. Their only option is to dodge the furious fur-balls and escape in their rockets (the 'Rocket' of the title). Your job is to guide the panicky critters rocket-wards to freedom!

Guiding the ChuChus is simple enough. They run in a straight line and turn right when they hit a wall, so you need to place directional arrows on the squares to make them change direction when they run over them. You're limited to placing three arrows at a time, and if a KapuKapu hits an arrow twice then it magically disappears. The harder the levels, the more ChuChus and KapuKapus and internal walls you have to deal with, and the game becomes a frantic, action-packed joy even though you're literally just placing arrows on a board. Simple and hopelessly compulsive gaming.

There are a number of ways to play, including Puzzle mode where you can create your own board.

WAYS TO PLAY TODAY

RETRO RATING 5/5

iOS
ChuChu Rocket! Universe is a revived and updated version that now boasts 3D graphics and gameplay that literally add an extra dimension to this ace puzzle game.

? *ChuChu Rocket!* was partly developed to showcase the Dreamcast's new abilities, with the developers wanting to get 100 sprites pinging around the screen at once.

SONY TIMELINE

Despite being relatively late to the console party, Sony took it by storm with an absolute game-changer, and then followed it up with several more...

1994
PlayStation
The big turning point where gaming also became an acceptable adult pursuit.

2000
PlayStation 2
More power, and the added ability to play these new-fangled things known as 'DVDs'.

2004
PSP
Sony's ace handheld device that went head-to-head with the DS (again, don't mention the battery life).

GALACTIC GAMING
In 1993 Russian cosmonaut Aleksandr Serebrov became the first person to play a video game in space when he took his Game Boy and a copy of *Tetris* with him on a mission.

POLAROID PICTURE

Before camera phones, if you wanted to see a photo as soon as you'd taken it, you needed a Polaroid camera – a square-shaped snap was spat out before your eyes! Inventor Edwin H. Land had the idea for it because his three-year-old daughter couldn't grasp why she couldn't see the photos immediately.

2006

PlayStation 3

More games!
Blu-rays!
Online gaming!
The future started here.

2011

PS Vita

A great unit, but it struggled to compete with the Nintendo 3DS and the rise of mobile gaming.

BIG SPLASH

Both the Super Soaker and the Nerf Gun were invented by a former NASA engineer named Lonnie Johnson. He reportedly used the Super Soaker during an important meeting with the company that manufactured it. Well, how else would you show what it does?

INTERSTELLAR INSPIRATION

The iPod was named by copywriter Vinnie Chieco after the design reminded him of the film *2001: A Space Odyssey* and the famous line, 'Open the pod bay doors, Hal!' By amazing coincidence the iPod was released in 2001.

PLAYSTATION GAMES

CRASH BANDICOOT

WHAT'S IT ALL ABOUT?

It would be madness to even consider launching a console without its own platform-based megastar, and Sony certainly didn't disappoint. Say a big 'hello' to Crash Bandicoot!

Much like Mario in the Mushroom Kingdom, Crash has a rescue mission to complete. Doctor Neo Cortex (a scientist who is, you guessed it, up to no good) has been brainwashing the local wildlife to become part of his army. Crash was made of stern stuff, though, and couldn't be washed, so the bad doctor dumped him on an island and tried to work his evil magic on Crash's one true love, Tawna, who now needs rescuing. Standing in Crash's way is the aforementioned army and various bosses. The platform action shifts from 3D to side-scrolling on occasion, and there are power-ups and bonuses galore.

Crash Bandicoot does a terrific job of setting up its own world, its own style, its own sense of humour, and its own unique take on the platform genre. It simply takes what works and makes sure that you have a whole heap of fun experiencing it, with lots to explore over the 25 levels and plenty of villains to jump on. Possibly the most fun game to crash on to the PS One.

Crash unleashes his signature spin attack that takes down any baddie daft enough to get near him.

WAYS TO PLAY TODAY

RETRO RATING 5/5

PlayStation 4
Crash and his pals got a shiny HD update in 2017 and the original game, plus its two equally awesome sequels, can be purchased for the PS4.

RETRO RATING 4/5

iOS and Android
The classic Crash style of leaping-and-a-spinning has been nicely translated to mobile devices in the form of *Crash Bandicoot: On the Run!* (The exclamation mark is both part of the title and an indication of our excitement!)

RETRO RATING 4/5

Nintendo Switch
Need more Crash in your gaming life? If so, grab yourself a copy of the brilliant *Skylanders Imaginators*, which features a guest appearance from the ace bandicoot.

? The development team were certain they wanted a furry creature for the PS One's signature platform outing but took their time choosing one. And for a while 'Willie the Wombat' was frontrunner!

PLAYSTATION GAMES

WIPEOUT 2097

WHAT'S IT ALL ABOUT?

It's back to the future we go for more anti-gravity racing. Where these supersonic racers are going, they don't need roads...

WipEout 2097 picks up about 40 years after the original *WipEout,* with the F3600 anti-gravity racing league now upgraded to a far more speedy and dangerous form – the F5000 AG racing league. The basics are still the same though, as you take control of your craft and attempt to pilot it to anti-gravity glory over a series of increasingly difficult tracks and racing classes. Unlike most other racing games, a bit of aggro is essential to taking the chequered flag, and there are a range of weapons on offer to destroy your opponents' shields and send them packing.

The racetracks are terrifically satisfying to get to grips with and feature plenty of high-speed straights, tricky corner sections and dips. Key to navigating these is the 'air brake' system – once you master this, zipping round even the tightest bends becomes a breeze. You also have to choose your fighting tactics wisely – although it's tempting to try to win by bumping off as many craft as you can find, this is surprisingly time-consuming. All this is topped off with a soundtrack made up of suitably fast-paced bangers. Strap in for what is probably the coolest game of all time!

There are four different classes of craft on offer – Vector, Venom, Rapier and Phantom. Vector is the easiest, and Phantom is the fastest!

WAYS TO PLAY TODAY

RETRO RATING 4/5

PlayStation 4
Although it doesn't include the instalment you see here, *WipEout Omega Collection* bundles together the PS3's *WipEout HD Fury* and the PS Vita's *WipEout 2048*. And both are high-octane fun!

WipEout 2097 was compatible with the NeGon controller. This was a strange-looking piece of motion-based tech that you could twist, making it perfect for working the air-brake system.

187

PARAPPA THE RAPPER

WHAT'S IT ALL ABOUT?

Comin' straight outta the PlayStation is a crazy little dog called PaRappa! Join the rhyme-master general as he attempts to win over Sunny Funny via the medium of rap.

You'd be hard pushed to find a simpler game. Press the buttons on your controller in the right order and in time to some catchy tunes. But sometimes simple is best, simple is compelling, and simple is insanely fun – which is what you get here. PaRappa's quest to win over the girl of his dreams takes in karate lessons, learning to drive, baking a cake and taking to the stage at Club Fun – all with a whole lotta rappin' goin' on.

There are essentially six levels and in each one, someone will rap and you have to respond by pressing the buttons that pop up on screen. Press the correct buttons at the right time and the 'U Rappin' meter will rank your performance as 'Good' or 'Cool', but wrong words and poor timing result in a 'Bad' or 'Awful' rating. Only good and cool rappers get to progress. You do need to get a feel for each song rather than just rely on reacting swiftly to the on-screen prompts, but once you get into the swing of it there will be no stopping you. It's a rapper's delight.

PaRappa's first stop is the karate dojo to learn from the legendary Chop Chop Master Onion.

Expert timing is what's needed to gain that all-important 'U rappin' GOOD' rating.

WAYS TO PLAY TODAY

RETRO RATING 4/5

PlayStation 4
PaRappa the Rapper was popular enough for a spin-off game (Um Jammer Lammy) and a sequel. And to celebrate its 20th anniversary it received the HD remaster treatment for the PS4, which you can get your paws on today.

? 'PaRappa' is a play on the Japanese words for 'paper thin' and is a reference to the design of the characters.

COLIN MCRAE RALLY

WHAT'S IT ALL ABOUT?

Rallying is very much the opposite to on-track racing in almost every sense. Forget about super-sleek machines and precision driving, it's time to chuck the car about and kick up some dirt!

It's just you and the car (and your co-driver) versus the course (and the clock). *Colin McRae Rally* keeps things uncomplicated, and ditches any sort of story to focus on slamming the pedal to the metal and tearing around the various courses as quickly as you can. There are eight rallies in the game, all with their own particular obstacles to overcome (such as ice or driving at night), and you have 12 cars to choose from that are grouped into three difficulty levels. And from there, you're off!

Even though there are no other cars to contend with out on the roads, the action is still thrilling. The feel of the different cars and the various surfaces have been captured to what we assume is a hugely realistic degree, and it's immensely fun hurling your car through the turns and wheel-spinning and power-sliding to your heart's content. The controls are super-easy to get used to but the later stages and higher-powered vehicles present a real challenge. It's the ultimate in dirt-based driving.

This is what happens when you don't listen to your co-driver's instructions!

WAYS TO PLAY TODAY

RETRO RATING 5/5

PlayStation 4 and Xbox One

Colin McRae Rally eventually morphed into the superb *DIRT* series, and like a lot of sports games is updated on a regular basis. So the original game you see here may not be available but the *DIRT* series most definitely is! Number 5 has been saddled with a 12 rating, but previous outings are rated 3.

? *CMR* features a fantastic Easter Egg. Activate a cheat code on one of the night-time stages and your car gets abducted by aliens!

PLAYSTATION 2 GAMES

RATCHET & CLANK

WHAT'S IT ALL ABOUT?

It's platform time again! And it's a Lombax and a robot who are leaping to the rescue. Join the dynamic duo on an interplanetary caper that you'll never forget.

After Mario, Sonic, Crash, Kirby, Banjo and Kazooie you may be wondering if there's room for yet more cartoon-y characters jumping about the place in a desperate attempt to save their world. Of course there is! This stuff never gets old. Furry humanoid creature Ratchet is a mechanic whose day is interrupted by the arrival of Clank, who's on a mission to stop a corrupt businessman from planet Blarg harvesting and destroying other inhabited planets.

In among the usual super-fun jumping, baddie-bashing and power-up collecting, there's great interplay between the two characters. Clank is mostly hitching a ride on Ratchet's back, but as the game progresses his abilities get upgraded and he plays more of a solo role in the 20 or so missions that need completing. The levels offer loads of variety, from racing to space combat and mini games. This iconic platform title is well worth jumping on board with!

Ratchet can make use of 36 different weapons and gadgets that are dotted around the levels.

If you prefer, you can shift to a first-person perspective to take in your surroundings.

WAYS TO PLAY TODAY

RETRO RATING 4/5

PlayStation 4
As with a lot of games from this era, *Ratchet & Clank* has been given the upgrade treatment and is now available on the PS4 in shiny new HD form.

RETRO RATING 5/5

Playstation 5
Ratchet & Clank: Rift Apart is the duo's latest (and possibly greatest?) rip-roaring adventure, with loads of new weapons and assorted awesome-ness to discover.

> The development team shared game tech with the boffins behind *Jak and Daxter: The Precursor Legacy*, and each game contains subtle shout-outs to the other.

193

PLAYSTATION 2 GAMES

SSX TRICKY

WHAT'S IT ALL ABOUT?

It's snow joke out there on the mountains, with hordes of dudes demanding you pull off ever-more death-defying moves and conquer super-steep courses. Strap on your board and head out to the slopes!

Like a boarder-cross rider who's just seen the starting gate drop, *SSX Tricky* leaps straight into the action. And like all good sports sims it focuses on putting you right there in the athlete's shoes (or chunky boots in this case). The main World Circuit mode sees you compete with other riders over ten different tracks, with clashes split into two major categories: Race and Show-off. The former is all about finishing first (obvs), and the latter is trick central, with the most outlandish manoeuvres winning you the big points.

Also on hand are Practice, Single Event and Freeride modes (the last giving you the opportunity to shred the mountains without any bothersome competition nonsense).

The control system will be familiar to anyone who's played these sorts of games before and has been nicely tailored to fit the mechanics of snowboarding. The mountains and courses all have distinct designs and offer up loads of different routes and obstacles to perform tricks off. The moves on offer are just the right blend of realistic and outlandish. Check it out.

Night-time levels let you show off your moves under the stars.

Bustin' out a classic method air!

WAYS TO PLAY TODAY

RETRO RATING 4/5

Xbox One
SSX went on to have a fair few sequels, and the version that landed on the Xbox 360 is up for grabs via Xbox Live. The graphics and sound are much improved and the gameplay is as fun as it ever was.

? The 2012 reboot was originally going to be titled *SSX: Deadly Descents*, but that idea was ditched when it was pointed out that it would make the action too serious and take all the fun out of the game.

PLAYSTATION 2 GAMES

PRO EVOLUTION SOCCER 6

WHAT'S IT ALL ABOUT?

All the teams, tournaments, grounds and questionable refereeing decisions that you could ever want. And none of that pesky VAR either! This is football at its finest.

As with *SSX Tricky*, there's no messing around when that whistle blows for kick off. Choose your team (on a domestic or international setting) and get busy scoring! There are lots of real-life teams, players and stadiums to choose from, and they're all tweaked to reflect their real-life counterparts to offer up different playing experiences in both one- and two-player modes.

And what an experience it is! Realism has always been at the heart of good sport sims, and *Pro Evo* goes the extra mile. It has a super-nifty random element whereby taking the same kick or the same tackle in the same way won't always achieve the same result. A free kick can either slam into the top corner or bash against the woodwork depending on if a player is having a good (virtual) day or not. The AI of the players you don't control is top-notch, with both defence and offence behaving as you'd expect to see on *Match of the Day*. The beautiful game just got a bit more beautiful.

Each team's real-life playing styles have been modelled in the game for added realism.

Uh oh! Looks like Mr Blue's been up to no good!

WAYS TO PLAY TODAY

RETRO RATING 5/5

PlayStation 4 and Xbox One

Unsurprisingly, given its name, *Pro Evo* has continued to evolve over the years before morphing into the *eFootball* series. As with most other sports sims the older versions are still worth a play and are dead cheap secondhand.

RETRO RATING 4/5

iOS and Android

If mobile football fun is more your type of thing, head over to whichever app store you favour to find a thumping version of *eFootball PES 2021* to download.

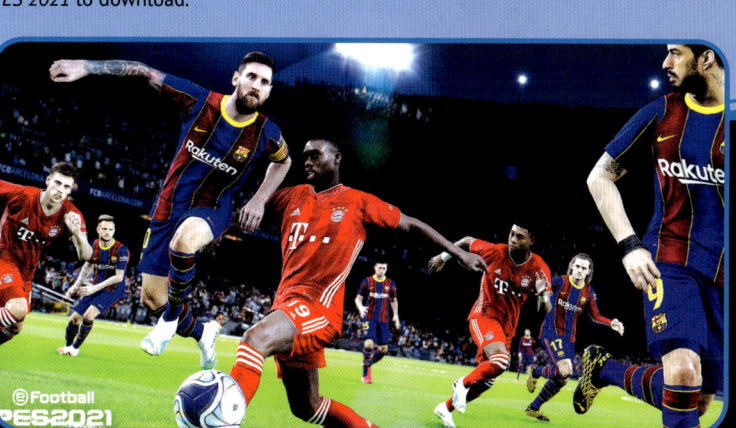

If you don't like the regular footie strips on offer and fancy something a bit more special, then head to the PES Shop where you can kit your team out in ostrich, penguin or dinosaur costumes!

GAMECUBE GAMES

THE LEGEND OF ZELDA: THE WIND WAKER

WHAT'S IT ALL ABOUT?

After traipsing around the green, green grass of Hyrule time after time, Link has decided he needs a change. He has set sail on a nautical adventure, traversing the high seas and larking about with some pirates!

It's quite a change seeing Link giving Hyrule the heave-ho and sailing off over the horizon, and it's also one that works brilliantly. The adventure begins with Link back in his childhood home on Outlet Island where a giant bird has nabbed his sister and the only way he can rescue her is by teaming up with a pirate and setting sail on his talking ship, the King of the Red Lions. This is made easier by having the Wind Waker to hand, which is a musical instrument that alters the direction of the wind. As with all Zelda games there's way more to it than that, and the adventure takes in exploration and combat in and on all manner of dungeons, mountains, islands, oceans and side quests.

The world on offer here is once again vast, and a joy to navigate. The slow nature of sailing the ship means you get to take in every detail and immerse yourself in the islands and oceans. And it's still easy to visit the places that are crucial to the story as the map highlights the most important locations. It's not all plain sailing, though, as there's plenty of puzzle-solving and fighting to be had along the way. A truly classic quest.

A sword, a shield and the beckoning call of the blue ocean is all Link needs for an adventure.

WAYS TO PLAY TODAY

RETRO RATING 4/5

Nintendo Wii U
Despite its popularity and classic status *The Wind Waker* still hasn't made its way to the Switch (although there are rumours…). However, if you have access to the underrated Wii U, there's an HD version of Link's watery adventure.

? There was originally a plan to have an island shaped like a GameCube, but this was abandoned. However, the basic idea was later revived for 'Dee Ess Island' in *Phantom Hourglass* on the DS.

GAMECUBE GAMES

ANIMAL CROSSING

WHAT'S IT ALL ABOUT?

If you've ever found the vast worlds that most games offer to be a bit overwhelming and would prefer to, say, pay off a mortgage on a cosy little house in a quiet sleepy village, look no further!

Animal Crossing is a haven. It's a world away from evil scientists, marauding aliens, reckless platform leaping and the relentless sounds of laser blasts. There are no poorly driven cars and no over-excitable sports people. There's just the calm of arriving in a village, moving into a lovely home, and settling into local life with a load of friendly talking animals. What could be better?

Living peacefully really is the goal of this game. You can choose which day-to-day tasks you perform, from writing letters, to doing a spot of decorating, and visiting your mates in nearby villages for a natter and some trading (the bills won't pay themselves, after all). The game runs in real-time – even when you don't have the console switched on. Play during the day and the village is buzzing with life, then switch on in the evening and the shops are all shut. Even the seasons change. All games are essentially about escaping, but this one gives you an escape from the stresses and strains of modern gaming too. Feel the calm.

Just another day hanging with your purple pal in the most tranquil virtual village you'll ever encounter.

WAYS TO PLAY TODAY

RETRO RATING 4/5

iOS and Android
Animal Crossing: Pocket Camp brings the great outdoors to your mobile device of choice, and gives you all the tools you need to create and decorate the campsite of your wildest dreams.

RETRO RATING 5/5

Nintendo Switch
The game has continued to evolve since its debut on the GameCube, and the latest version – *Animal Crossing: New Horizons* – can be bought for the Switch.

Animal Crossing was designed by Katsuya Eguchi, who wanted to create a game that captured the feeling of loneliness that came from moving to a new town where he didn't know anyone. Thankfully the finished game is a tad more upbeat!

GAMECUBE GAMES

SUPER MONKEY BALL

WHAT'S IT ALL ABOUT?

There are monkeys, they're in balls, and it's super — yes, it's *Super Monkey Ball*! We guarantee you'll go bananas as you take a roll through this awesome game.

Super Monkey Ball is one of those super easy to play and almost impossible to put down games that come along every now and then to ensnare every type of gamer. The aim is to tilt a platform to roll a monkey in a ball through a maze and towards a goal without tipping the unfortunate ape off the side. The more levels you complete, the harder they get, with some devilish multi-platform routes popping up later in the game. There are three difficulty levels with a host of play modes to vary the action – all nestled alongside a handful of ball-related mini games (billiards, bowling and golf – all with monkeys!).

Perhaps best of all is the multiplayer option, which allows four of you to either take turns guiding your primate of choice through the checkerboard platform-scapes, or play simultaneously in Party mode, where you can race, fight or launch the monkeys at a target. All this is topped off with eye-popping graphics and suitably simian sound effects. Grab a copy at the earliest opportunity – you'll have a ball!

Grab the bananas and head for the goal – it's a simple life being a super monkey (in a ball).

The routes get way narrower and waaaay trickier the further you get into the game.

WAYS TO PLAY TODAY

RETRO RATING 5/5

Nintendo Switch, PlayStation 4 and Xbox One

Super Monkey Ball spawned a huge number of spin-offs and sequels, the latest of which is *Banana Mania*. The mega gameplay is still intact, and is now spread out over 300 levels, 12 mini games and the usual multiplayer mode.

RETRO RATING 4/5

iOS and Android

Although it's not quite as highly regarded as its grown-up console-based brothers, there's a pretty good free version of *Super Monkey Ball* available in app form as part of the *Sega Forever* collection.

? When *Monkey Ball* first appeared in arcade form you controlled the movements of your monkey pals with a banana-shaped joystick. What else?!

GAME BOY ADVANCE GAMES

METROID FUSION

❗ WHAT'S IT ALL ABOUT?

If you thought Game Boy games were all brightly coloured, happy affairs set in cartoon-ish worlds with lots of cheery animals, take a look at this dark chapter in the *Metroid* series! It's the most tense and atmospheric game you'll ever hold in your soon-to-be-sweaty palms...

You'd think that after seeing off the dastardly Space Pirates and their organic weapon, the Metroids, Samus Aran would take at least a few days off. But she's straight back with a group of (non-evil) scientists to survey the Metroids' home planet. As bad luck would have it, she's infected with an X Parasite, crashes her ship on the return journey, has her infected Power Suit surgically removed, and is only saved by being injected with cells from the remaining Metroids. And, she also has a new nemesis in the form of SA-X, who came to life from her infected Power Suit. Perhaps the sofa and Netflix would have been a better option after all...

SA-X basically mimics Samus at full power, meaning that the game is based around a weakened Samus being stalked by a more powerful version of herself! See what we mean about this being tense?! The action has the same feel as the SNES version but is way more linear and less free-roaming, which makes sense as the emphasis is less on exploring and more on stalking and being stalked by SA-X. There are also plenty of other enemies to take on with Samus' signature moves. You'll be hard-pushed to find other GBA games of this calibre.

A weakened Samos Aran explores her grimy surroundings.

WAYS TO PLAY TODAY

RETRO RATING 4/5

Nintendo Wii U
If you want to go head-to-parasitic-head with SA-X, you're going to need a Wii U. Othewise, just head to the Metroid Hub on nintendo.co.uk where there are plenty of Samus Aran adventures on offer.

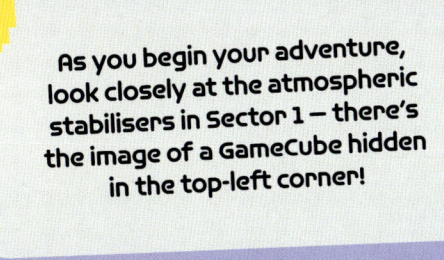

? As you begin your adventure, look closely at the atmospheric stabilisers in Sector 1 – there's the image of a GameCube hidden in the top-left corner!

GAME BOY ADVANCE GAMES

MARIO VS DONKEY KONG

WHAT'S IT ALL ABOUT?

An Italian plumber versus a giant ape is an unlikely match-up, but it's also the greatest and possibly longest-running feud in gaming! What could they possibly still have to get aggro about, you may ask? Well...

In a way it's nice to see that all these years later that Mazza and old Donkey-chops still haven't sorted out their differences. Although here it's a whole new difference that they're bickering over. Mario has set up his own toy company making 'Mini-Mario' action figures. Donkey Kong becomes a tad obsessed with them but can't get his mucky paws on any as they've sold out, so it's off to the factory he goes to pinch a load for himself. Mario's having none of it, though, and is in hot pursuit to recover his stock (and no doubt to educate the ape in the wonders of pre-ordering).

The action is basically an updated take on the platform-and-puzzle-solving that the original did so well. Mario has a whole new set of moves (including backflips, triple jumps and handstands) that are all vital to master if you want to progress. The levels are also structured so that you have to find a key to a locked door, rescue a Mini Mario, and then, once you've found six, guide them to a toy box before taking on the great ape himself in a boss battle. It gives the game a great balance in both action and difficulty, and there are numerous references to the original game to spot along the way. Long may this rivalry last.

A plumber, an ape and some platforms — some things never get old!

WAYS TO PLAY TODAY

RETRO RATING 4/5

Nintendo Wii U
The original version of the game you see here is still available if you happen to have a Wii U to hand.

? Originally a level editor was to be included in the game but unfortunately it was scrapped. However, there are rumours it remains in a partial form and can be awakened with a cheat code…

RETRO QUIZ! ANSWERS

1 c. The Rock

2 a. A square

3 b. Princess

4 a. Pikachu

5 c. Shade

6 a. Banjo

7 c. *Gauntlet*

8 a. Tails

9 a. Bass fishing

10 c. A rapper

11 c. *Super Monkey Ball*

12 b. SB388

13 b. Blibby Blab-blub

14 b. Just his pants, and nothing else